PRAISE FOR
KEYS TO FINANCIAL EXCELLENCE

"*Keys to Financial Excellence* by Phil Pringle reveals that the secret to a life of abundance in all areas of our lives is a willingness to give to God and others. When we offer ourselves and our finances with loving spirits and open hands, we touch the heart of God, and His grace overflows. Read this book to be blessed and to be a blessing."

—*Joyce Meyer*
Best-selling author and Bible teacher

"God's blessings are released when we give from generous and willing hearts. *Keys to Financial Excellence,* by my friend Pastor Phil Pringle, reveals God's desire not only to meet our needs, but also to pour out His abundance. Topics such as the blessing of tithing, debt cancellation, the laws of giving, and sowing to the Spirit will awaken in you a desire to transform the world through the power of giving."

—*John Bevere*
Best-selling author

"It's always a great pleasure to read material that has been tried and proven by the author. Phil Pringle is one of those leaders of a rare breed who writes from the fiery furnace of experience. He has sown these principles of financial wisdom into countless thousands of people and hundreds of churches. *Keys to Financial Excellence* will change your financial life if you put them into practice. This material is great for all levels of people: the business person, the person seeking to get out of debt, the pastor who has vision but not enough resources, the young person who desires to set his financial path before him, and the giver in every church who desires to go to another level of giving and receiving. This book is a winner. It's trustworthy, biblical, practical, and inspirational."

—*Frank Damazio*
City Bible Church

PRAISE FOR
KEYS TO FINANCIAL EXCELLENCE

"Keys to Financial Excellence isn't a book written from an ideological perspective—it's the real stuff, tried and proven."
—*John C. Maxwell*
Best-selling author

"Phil Pringle is a true leader of leaders. He has a fresh, unique way of looking at everything, and there is a strong anointing on his life and ministry. He writes from a wealth of knowledge and experience. This book is certainly deserving of our attention."
—*Pastor Rick Shelton*
Senior Minister, Life Christian Center
St. Louis, Missouri

"Phil Pringle has been at the forefront of radical church leadership for many years. At Christian City Church, he has pioneered many different areas of ministry, gleaning valuable insight and wisdom along the way."
—*Pastor Colin Dye*
Senior Minister, Kensington Temple
London, England

"Inspiring, thought-provoking, challenging."
—*Russell Evans*
Director, Planet Shakers, South Australia

"The importance of a book like this cannot be overstated. The keys that are contained in these pages have the power to unlock the windows of heaven over individual lives and the church as a whole. I encourage the reader to absorb not only the content of this book, but also the spirit of its author and to enter into the abundance of riches that God has for your life."
—*Dr. Dick Bernal*
Senior Minister, Jubilee Christian Center
San Jose, California

PHIL PRINGLE

KEYS
to
FINANCIAL EXCELLENCE

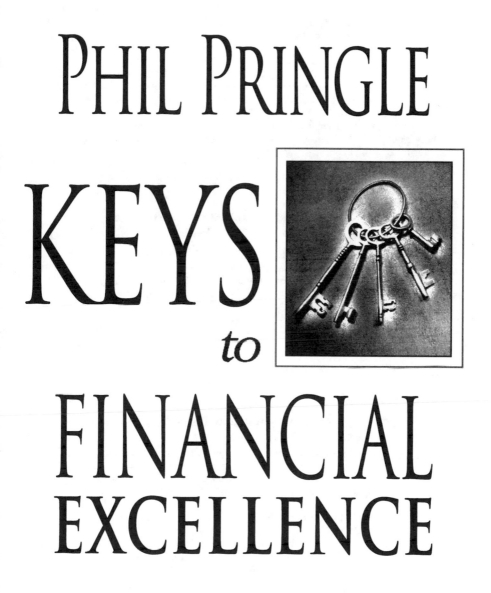

WHITAKER
HOUSE

KEYS TO FINANCIAL EXCELLENCE

Phil Pringle
Christian City Church Oxford Falls, Australia
website: www.ccc.org.au

ISBN-13: 978-0-88368-800-7
ISBN-10: 0-88368-800-X
Printed in the United States of America
Australia: © 2003 in by Pax Ministries Pty Ltd.
United States of America: © 2005 by Phil Pringle

1030 Hunt Valley Circle
New Kensington, PA 15068
www.whitakerhouse.com

Library of Congress Cataloging-in-Publication Data
Pringle, Phil, 1952–
Keys to financial excellence / Phil Pringle.
p. cm.
Summary: "Provides readers with biblical truths and principles of prosperity that can be applied to all areas of their lives"—Provided by publisher.
Includes bibliographical references.
ISBN-13: 978-0-88368-800-7 (hardcover : alk. paper)
ISBN-10: 0-88368-800-X (hardcover : alk. paper)
1. Wealth—Religious aspects—Christianity. 2. Finance, Personal—Religious aspects—Christianity. 3. Christian giving. 4. Tithes. I. Title.
BR115.W4P75 2005
241'.68—dc22   2005010468

ACKNOWLEDGMENTS

For years, leaders have been asking me for copies of the messages I use in our church for raising finances. My friends have also urged me to write on the matter. I was going to call this book *52 Reasons to Give* in an effort to encourage believers to give at least once every week of the year. However, that seemed too restrictive. I easily could have ended up with 365 reasons to give, or a thousand reasons to give; so I settled on *Keys to Financial Excellence*.

Giving is intrinsic to the nature of God. As His children, giving needs to be basic to our nature, as well. My prayer is that this book will not just be messages for leaders to use, but will also be inspirational to every believer who reads it. I pray it will not just provide some teaching about giving, but will also actually cause people to give at greater levels so that churches and ministries everywhere will prosper because of it.

Thanks to all my friends who regularly pestered me about when this book was to be published. Thanks to our incredible congregation, who have inspired Chris and me with their generosity and willingness of heart to give sacrificially over the years. They have enabled us to do an amazing amount of great things for God, including the reality that we now occupy a debt-free suite of buildings worth over sixty million dollars.

Thanks to my PA, Di Payne, who assists me at every level in helping me run my life, to June Henning for originally getting this book off the ground, and to Jesse Allen for keeping all of our Pax projects on track; without you, books like this would never make it out of my computer.

Thanks to our phenomenal ministry team at Christian City Church Oxford Falls, who live the adventure of a generous life.

Thanks to our kids who have had to give in sharing their parents with a thousand other people over the years. Their great attitude in this has helped us help build the lives of others.

Thanks to my beautiful wife, Chris, who has made generous sacrifices, given joyfully, and stood together with me when we decided to give our cash-in-hand salary over five years toward our building fund. What a gal!

Finally, as this new hardback edition of *Keys to Financial Excellence* goes to press in the U.S., I wish to thank Whitaker House for the hard work that they have invested in furthering our vision and to Michael McCall for shaping the existing text into an upgraded format for today's readers.

—*Phil Pringle*
Sydney, Australia

CONTENTS

FOREWORD

I f we are to achieve the purposes that God has for the church in this world, it is imperative that we break out of a poverty mind-set into a liberal and bountiful attitude about money and giving where the abundance of heaven can freely flow. The enemy is trying desperately to bind the church of God through this mind-set of poverty and an epidemic of cynicism regarding the whole area of finances in the church.

Thank God there are some preachers like Phil Pringle who are prepared to step boldly and unapologetically into the fullness of what the Word of God has to say about money, prosperity, and the power of giving. His revelation of the abundance of God and how that is released through a willingness to give generously to God has become a hallmark of his increasingly influential ministry.

Indeed, the things he has achieved in God through his own ministry are a testimony to the truth of this revelation. Christian City Church in Sydney, Australia, where Dr. Pringle is Senior Minister, is a thriving and prosperous church and is widely renowned for its generous spirit. This church has seen God perform some incredible miracles of provision through the sacrificial but enthusiastic giving of its membership. Many other churches and individuals around the world—both within the Christian City Church movement and beyond— have also experienced great blessing through Dr. Pringle's preaching and teaching about finances and giving.

The importance of a book like this cannot be overstated. The keys that are contained in these pages have the power to unlock the windows of heaven over individual lives and the church as a whole. I encourage you to absorb not only the content of this book, but also the spirit of its author and to enter into the abundance of riches that God has for your life.

—*Dr. Dick Bernal*
Senior Minister, Jubilee Christian Center
San Jose, California

FOUNDATIONS OF ABUNDANT LIVING

KEY #1

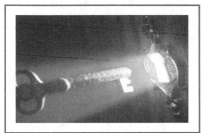

THE WAYS OF GOD ARE NOT THE WAYS OF MAN

"For My thoughts are not your thoughts, nor are your ways My ways," says the LORD.
—Isaiah 55:8

God seeks to *give*. Man seeks to *get*. Giving is God's way. Getting is man's way. If we truly desire to live close to God and be more like Him, then we must begin by giving.

*God so loved the world that He **gave**...*
(John 3:16, emphasis added)

Mankind seeks to obtain and increase its money, food, clothes, possessions, houses, lands and businesses by expending energy in *getting* more and more "things." In the kingdom of God, Christ doesn't have a problem with our obtaining material possessions, but He does tell us that the way to gain them is not by getting but by giving:

*Therefore do not worry, saying, "What shall we eat?"
or "What shall we drink?" or "What shall we wear?"
For after all these things the Gentiles seek. For your
heavenly Father knows that you need all these things.
But **seek first** the kingdom of God and His righteousness, **and all these things shall be added to
you**.* (Matthew 6:31–33, emphasis added)

As Jesus Himself tells us in the verse above, when we
focus on seeking the ways of God (being a *giver*), material
possessions *will be given to us*.
No need to go out and struggle
to get them in our own power;
God will do the getting as we do
the giving.

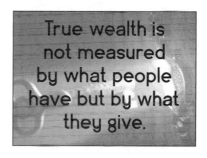

Giving is giving—period.
Paying people for work they do
for you is not giving. Putting
something into someone's hands
with conditions attached is not giving. Loaning to someone
is not giving.

Giving is completely relinquishing control of something
of yours into the control of another person to do with as he
pleases.

True wealth is not measured by what people *have* but by
what they give *in proportion* to what they have.

*Now Jesus sat opposite the treasury and saw how the
people put money into the treasury. And many who
were rich put in much. Then one poor widow came
and threw in two mites....So He called His disciples*

to Himself and said to them, "Assuredly, I say to you that this poor widow has put in more than all those who have given to the treasury; for they all put in out of their abundance, but she out of her poverty put in all that she had." (Mark 12:41–44)

Fortunately, everyone is capable of giving *something.* Even the simplest of things can become a gift to someone in need. If we meet someone who has a frown on her face, we can give her our smile. If someone is without food, we can share our meal with him. However, the measure of a truly godly giver is in going *above and beyond,* as the widow did in Mark 12:42. How much you want to receive of God's abundant blessings is in direct proportion to how much you give back of the blessings He has bestowed upon you. The more you give, the more you will receive. Likewise, the more you receive, the more you should *desire* to give.

———◆———

Jesus did *not* say that if we are given much, then "some" will be required from us or "a little" will be required from us, but *much* will be required from us:

For everyone to whom much is given, from him much will be required. (Luke 12:48)

Winston Churchill put it in a nutshell: "We make a living by what we get. We make a *life* by what we give."

The legacy you build will not be based on what you accumulate for yourself. Rather, you will be remembered for what you have *given.*

KEY #2

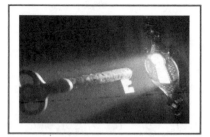

THE ATTITUDE
OF GIVING

...Your generous Spirit.
—Psalm 51:12

G iving is an *attitude* before it becomes an action. The Holy Spirit is a Person with a generous, giving attitude.

To be giving or generous is to have a joyful spirit: Giving people are joyful people! When we are filled with the Holy Spirit, we too are generous and giving, because *giving* is the Christian way.

People who have a giving attitude don't stop to calculate the cost when a need presents itself. If they have the resources, they simply find themselves giving—it's a natural response.

On the other hand, being cheap, miserly, or stingy, or giving out of grudging obligation, are not giving attitudes and are not what God wants from us (although they are often dressed up and paraded as Christian piety).

———◆———

Giving means being willing and cheerful when we release something of ours into the ownership of another.

In Exodus 35:5, Moses extended an invitation to *"whoever is of a willing heart"* to bring an offering to the Lord. In 2 Corinthians 9:7, Paul told the believers to give *"not grudgingly or of necessity; for God loves a cheerful giver."* Paul prepared the people to give with a proper attitude, so that when he received their offering it would not be a matter of grudging obligation but of cheerful celebration.

As Chuck Swindoll put it, "A happy spirit takes the grind out of giving. The grease of gusto frees the gears of generosity."

The following story by Valerie Cox illustrates how circumstances can reveal the state of our own generosity:

———◆———

"The Cookie Thief"

A woman was waiting at an airport one night,
with several long hours before her flight.
She hunted for a book in the airport shop,
bought a bag of cookies and found a place to drop.

She was engrossed in her book, but happened to see,
that the man beside her, as bold as could be,
grabbed a cookie or two from the bag between,
which she tried to ignore to avoid a scene.

She read, munched cookies, and watched the clock,
as the gutsy "cookie thief" diminished her stock.
She was getting more irritated as the minutes ticked by,
thinking, "If I weren't so nice, I'd blacken his eye!"

With each cookie she took, he took one too.
When only one was left, she wondered what he'd do.
With a smile on his face and a nervous laugh,
he took the last cookie and broke it in half.

He offered her half, as he ate the other.
She snatched it from him and thought, "Oh brother,
this guy has some nerve, and he's also rude.
Why, he didn't even show any gratitude!"

She had never known when she had been so galled,
and sighed with relief when her flight was called.
She gathered her belongings and headed for the gate,
refusing to look back at the "thieving ingrate."

She boarded the plane and sank in her seat,
then sought her book, which was almost complete.
As she reached in her baggage, she gasped with surprise:
There was her bag of cookies in front of her eyes!

"If mine are here," she moaned with despair,
"then the others were his, and he tried to share!"
Too late to apologize, she realized with grief,
that *she* was the rude one, the ingrate, the thief.

KEY #3

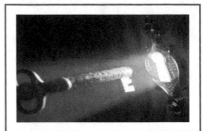

GENEROSITY: THE DOOR TO GREAT DESTINY

A generous man devises generous things, and by generosity he shall stand.
—Isaiah 32:8

G iving is one thing; generosity is another. We can be givers and still not be generous.

The kindhearted, merciful, non-condemning person easily gives far more than is expected, easily goes the extra mile, and easily exceeds what is required. It is the generous person, the *big-thinking* person, who thinks and acts in terms of better quality, larger quantity, and above-and-beyond giving.

The opposite of generosity is stinginess. Stingy people measure out the smallest, lowest-quality thing they can find in order to gratify their meager conscience. That is a legalistic mind-set that comprehends nothing about the generous Spirit of God.

The key to generosity is the Holy Spirit: To be filled with the Spirit is to overflow with generosity in our attitudes, with our possessions, with our money, and with ourselves.

The Bible gives many striking examples of overt generosity:

- ✓ King David generously showered wealth and property upon Mephibosheth, the crippled son of Saul's son Jonathan. In 2 Samuel 9:7–13, we learn that David not only had Mephibosheth eat at his table all the rest of his days, but he also gave him the entire estate of the late king Saul, plus all of the servants of Saul's house *and* all the income from Saul's vast properties!

- ✓ In Genesis 13:9, Abraham displayed extraordinary generosity when he gave to his nephew Lot all the plains of Jordan—half of all the lands that had been promised to Abraham by God Himself.

- ✓ In John 2:6–10, the generosity of Jesus was shown when He turned plain water into 180 gallons of the finest wine. He did this at the end of a feast, when neither that much wine nor the "best" wine was needed.

- ✓ In Acts 20:34–35, Paul was generous when he worked hard and prospered, and then supported everyone who was traveling with him. He explained that the reason for his generosity was so they would *"...remember the words of the Lord Jesus, that He said, 'It is more blessed to give than to receive.'"*

There are countless other biblical stories of *above and beyond* generosity. These examples were set for us to follow.

Enthusiastic, Willing-Hearted Generosity

Restore to me the joy of Your salvation, and uphold me by Your generous Spirit. (Psalm 51:12)

Generosity opens the doors to great destiny. Your generous spirit can expose incredible opportunities you might have never known God was offering you, blessings beyond your greatest desires and imagination.

My good friend and colleague Steve Janes (who oversees a number of Christian City Churches from our capital city, Canberra) inspired me with his insight into the example of Rebekah in Genesis 24. That amazing account followed Eliezer, chief servant of Abraham, as he traveled back to his master's homeland to find a wife for Abraham's son Isaac...

Eliezer took ten camels laden with gifts for the fortunate woman whom he would choose as Isaac's bride. As he approached a well just inside the homeland, he prayed that God would reveal the future wife of Isaac by her generosity:

Now let it be that the young woman to whom I say, "Please let down your pitcher that I may drink," and she says, "Drink, and I will also give your camels a drink"; let her be the one You have appointed for Your servant Isaac. And by this I will know that You have shown kindness to my master. (Genesis 24:14)

As soon as he has finished praying, along came Rebekah, the most beautiful young woman Eliezer had ever seen. When he asked her for a cup of water, without hesitation she gave him the water, and then she went above and beyond that act of generosity by also offering to water all of his camels!

So she said, "Drink, my lord." Then she quickly let her pitcher down to her hand, and gave him a drink. And when she had finished giving him a drink, she said, "I will draw water for your camels also, until they have finished drinking." Then she quickly emptied her pitcher into the trough, ran back to the well to draw water, and drew for all his camels.

(Genesis 24:18–20)

That was no small act of generosity. A camel can drink up to twenty-five gallons of water in one sitting. Also, the well was not some bucket-on-a-rope rig. She had to trudge some fifty steps down to the well to get the water. If each camel drank its fill, that would be two hundred and fifty gallons Rebekah had to lug all the way up those stairs—and she was not described as a beefy lass! At the very most, she could probably carry no more than five gallons 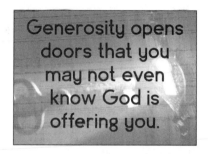 back up from the well at one time. That's fifty trips up and down those steps! Now *that* is generosity—eager, willing-hearted, hospitality in action.

> Generosity opens doors that you may not even know God is offering you.

Eliezer must have stood there drop-jawed at the sight of this beautiful young woman working her heart out—all from her unconditional, over-the-top generosity. And with each panting breath and faltering step, Rebekah was answering a prayer and marching toward a destiny far beyond her wildest dreams.

When she finished the task for Eliezer, he told her why he had come. Then Rebekah rushed and told her family the story, and her brother Laban ran out and invited Eliezer to their father's home. Within hours, the family, blessed with Eliezer's gifts, had agreed to the marriage of Rebekah to Isaac, and Rebekah was ready to depart on the journey to meet Isaac and his family—and to establish a legacy that is unmatched in all of human history.

The rest of the story is the foundation of the entire nation of Israel and of God's plan of salvation for mankind: Rebekah became the mother of Jacob (who became the father of the Israelite people, from whom Messiah would come), she became part of the wealthiest family in the entire East, and she went down in history as part of the plan of God to bring Christ into the world. All because of Rebekah's acts of selfless generosity. An incredible example!

The Bride of Christ

The beautiful story of Rebekah carries even more potent meanings for us today. Abraham is a picture of the Father; Isaac, of the Son; and Eliezer, of the Holy Spirit, who has been sent out into the world to find and prepare a bride for Jesus Christ. Enthusiastic, willing-hearted generosity is the first quality that God is looking for in the bride of Christ. The Holy Spirit comes with many different gifts from the Father for the bride, who opens the door to receiving those gifts through obediently serving the Holy Spirit in every way He prompts.

Let's commit to this attitude of generosity throughout our entire lives. Let's be ready at any time to give, to serve, and to be generous to whomever we meet and in whatever situation we find ourselves. That is how the door to great destiny opens before us!

KEY #4

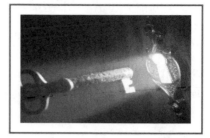

GREED

Then he said, "Beware! Don't be greedy for what you don't have. Real life is not measured by how much we own."
—Luke 12:15 NLT

When is enough, enough? In the movie *Wall Street*, the character Gordon Gecko, played by Michael Douglas, espoused what many consider the theme of the 1980s: *Greed is good*. Gecko's adversary asked him the question, "When is enough, enough—how many boats can you ski behind?"

Contentment remains the richest attitude we can possess. Contentment is *being happy*. If we think that our happiness depends on possessions we own, our status, success, or the size of our achievements, we will never be happy, because we will never own enough, achieve enough, or be important enough to satisfy those cravings. There is a point where we need to simply be happy as we are, to just accept our lives as they are and choose to *be happy*—no matter what we have or don't have.

Greed is *unrestrained desire*. It is excess instead of success. It is wanting ridiculously more than you need to have. Greed has been the downfall of too many people to even begin to name. It began with Adam and Eve wanting to eat from one tree when they had a million others to eat from. It is avaricious Laban deceiving his employee Jacob into reducing his wages ten times. It is Gehazi lying to get what his master turned down. Greed is *wanting what isn't yours*.

Greed twists character so that people increase the price of their services or products beyond what is reasonable and fair. Greed makes people ignore what they have, and seek those things they don't have and

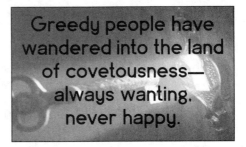

Greedy people have wandered into the land of covetousness— always wanting, never happy.

don't need. Greedy people have simply wandered into the land of covetousness, always wanting, never happy.

I have a friend who bought a piece of land that skyrocketed in value within weeks after the purchase. He was offered an incredible amount of money for it, but he declined, believing he could get still more. Someone else offered more. He held out believing he could get even more. After one year, however, prices crashed, and he eventually sold it for less than he paid for it. He had been offered a more than fair price for the property and could have made a handsome profit. But greed fouled his sound thinking.

Allow fairness to guide your thinking, and you will be able to make choices free of greed.

KEY #5

GIVING IS GOD'S WAY

Then Jesus lifted up His eyes, and seeing a great multitude coming toward Him, He said to Philip, "Where shall we buy bread, that these may eat?" But this He said to test him, for He Himself knew what He would do. Philip answered Him, "Two hundred denarii worth of bread is not sufficient for them, that every one of them may have a little." One of His disciples, Andrew, Simon Peter's brother, said to Him, "There is a lad here who has five barley loaves and two small fish."
—John 6:5–9

Occasionally, well-meaning people have approached me with schemes to raise money for the church. I have never felt comfortable about any of these. I must admit, though, that I have felt somewhat tempted. The raising of finances in church life is a continual burden on the leader. If there were some other way to accumulate wealth, it might make life easier, but my conviction has always been that *giving* is God's way.

———◆———

Some churches have bought into multilevel marketing businesses. These can be a great source of income for those who invest. However, when pastors and congregations get involved in these activities as a church fundraising strategy, relationships between the pastors and their congregations, and between the members of the congregations themselves, can quite easily become confused—*"Why are they suddenly so interested in me?"* Then, when the business proposition is announced, people become cynical and feel exploited, and relationships are compromised.

Giving is God's multilevel marketing plan for success.

But it is *giving* that is God's way, not business marketing. The members of the congregation are called to go out into the world, generate finances, and bring their offerings into church. In other words, they are called simply to give.

———◆———

In John 6, when Jesus asked His disciples how they were going to feed the multitude before them, they were dumbfounded. They had no idea. Yet a young boy gave what he had. It may seem like a very small gift in comparison to the size of the need. However, what is given into God's hands can become abundance through His supernatural power.

The disciples were no doubt feeling completely embarrassed as they began to hand out the one-twelfth portion of a sardine and bread bun they each had. There were five thousand men in front of them! If each man had a wife and three children, that made a total of *twenty-five thousand* people to feed!

Thomas probably got the tail end of a fish and a small crust. With two thousand people in front of him, I can imagine him holding his hands behind his back and telling the people to take as little as they could. However, they tug and pull and yank. He's too afraid to look. He gets to the end of the row and finds he's now holding a snapper and a French roll. He goes down the next row and finishes with a barracuda and an Italian loaf. By the end of the last row, people can't eat the swordfish he's dragging behind him—much less get through the pile of bread in his arms!

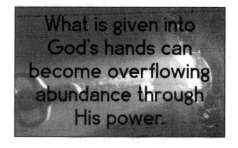

What is given into God's hands can become overflowing abundance through His power.

Through simple acts of giving, that meal multiplied. The boy gave, Jesus gave, the disciples gave, and in the end, there were twelve basketfuls left over! One basket for each disciple? Twelve baskets for the boy to take home to surprise Mom with? Whoever got those extra baskets of miracle meals, it was a great abundance!

KEY #6

GIVING MAN'S WAY: HOW NOT TO GIVE

By faith Abel offered to God a more excellent sacrifice than Cain, through which he obtained witness that he was righteous, God testifying of his gifts; and through it he being dead still speaks.
—Hebrews 11:4

Some people have the attitude that they'll give whatever they want. Those people usually resent any further calls made on them to give more, as if God should be happy He got anything from them at all. But, what we give and the way we give are to be according to God's way, because giving man's way never leads to blessings.

When we give to people, we prefer to choose the gift that is given. We tend to resent the receiver telling us what gift would be acceptable (especially when it's more than we anticipated giving them). But it's not always up to us to decide how much and in what way we are going to give.

Giving is not atonement for disobedience. We cannot avoid the requirements of God on our lives and at the same time claim that Jesus Christ is Lord over our lives. Many people refuse to tithe but give some other amount to God, based on their own criteria and arbitrary timing. But God has called us to tithe—period! The tithe is one-tenth of our income. We give that because Jesus is Lord. That means we do what He tells us to do—not just in some areas, but every area, including our finances.

Cheerful obedience in giving our one-tenth tithe isn't much to ask; it stands as an indication of our true heart toward God. Jesus did not grudgingly give one-tenth of His life for us; He gave it all. If we are 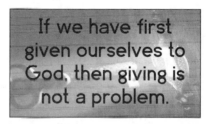 submitted to Him and claiming to serve Him, then we make ourselves available to Him to do whatever He asks of us. His will takes precedence over every area of our lives. When we bring our tithe to the Lord each week and sow from what He gives us, then we demonstrate that we are relinquishing control of our money to Him.

> *Concerning the ministering to the saints, it is superfluous for me to write to you; for I know your willingness, about which I boast of you to the Macedonians.*
> (2 Corinthians 9:1–2)

In 2 Corinthians 9, in an effort to provoke the Corinthian church to give generously, Paul boasts to them about the giving of the impoverished Macedonians. The reason the Macedonians were so free in giving was they had given themselves to the Lord *first*. If we, too, have given ourselves to God first, then giving is never a problem. However, if we have not given ourselves first to the Lord, then giving will always be a struggle.

The Story of Cain and Abel

It is incredible that the first murder ever in history was over *offerings*. This is not a light matter. There is incredible power in tithes and offerings. When ignored, people suffer. When respected, the power of God is unleashed in great blessing upon the individual and the entire church.

The story of Cain and Abel reveals this lordship. God has obviously told their parents, Adam and Eve, what must be given in offerings. In the garden, He had clothed the original couple with animal skins, in order to cover their nakedness after they had sinned. A life had to be taken (the slain animal) to provide this atonement covering for their sin.

However, when Cain brought his offering, he wanted to do it his way. He brought an offering of his own produce (a selection of vegetables), whereas his brother Abel brought a lamb from among his flocks. It's an interesting choice to sacrifice a carrot on the altar before God. But carrots don't bleed, and a *blood* sacrifice was what was called for. Therefore, God responded to Abel's sacrifice but not to Cain's. Maybe it was fire from heaven, or maybe it was less dramatic, but whatever happened, it aroused the worst of jealousies in Cain. Instead of repenting and bringing the kind of offering God asked for, he murdered Abel—his own brother!

Dishonest Giving: The Lesson of Ananias and Sapphira

But a certain man named Ananias, with Sapphira his wife, sold a possession. And he kept back part of the proceeds, his wife also being aware of it, and brought a certain part and laid it at the apostles' feet. But Peter said, "Ananias, why has Satan filled your heart to lie to the Holy Spirit and keep back part of the price of the land for yourself? While it remained, was it not your own? And after it was sold, was it not in your own control? Why have you conceived this thing in your heart? You have not lied to men but to God." Then Ananias, hearing these words, fell down and breathed his last. So great fear came upon all those who heard these things. (Acts 5:1–5)

The story of Ananias and Sapphira shows that we should never try to appear as though we are giving when we are not, or as though we are giving more than we actually are.

In the early days of the church, as the Holy Spirit moved powerfully throughout Jerusalem, people were selling their lands and houses and bringing the proceeds as offerings to the church. The apostles scrutinized each gift. Most people gave the entire income from the sale of their properties, but Ananias and Sapphira decided to secretly keep some of the money for themselves. They wanted to appear as though they were giving everything like everybody else was doing, so they told the apostle Peter that they were giving it all. But Peter discerned that they were lying—and both of them dropped dead in front of the entire assembly, one after the other!

I've known of churches that receive offerings for a minister and then withhold a portion of it (sometimes a large portion) without telling the people who gave or informing the minister who was to receive the offering. So, while the people believed they were giving to the ministry, a lot of their offering actually went to some other purpose. That is deceptive, and as the example of Ananias and Sapphira shows, it can be a deadly way to handle finances in the sight of God!

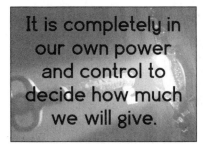

It is completely in our own power and control to decide how much we will give.

We must realize that it is completely in our own power to decide how much to give. Peter told the couple that it was up to them to choose the amount to donate to the church—they were never under compulsion to give one hundred percent. Their sin was that they proudly attempted to appear as though they were giving more than they actually were.

> *Pride goes before destruction, and a haughty spirit before a fall.* (Proverbs 16:18)

When we give, we must be honest and give what we say we will give.

PRINCIPLES OF PROSPERITY

Key #7

Abundance: The Authors of Scripture

You crown the year with Your goodness, and Your paths drip with abundance.
—Psalm 65:11

A bundance has always been a sign of the blessing of God. He is abundant toward His people. You may have heard it said that "God will supply only your need." That is not true. He will supply *more* than your need. Your cup will overflow so that you have abundance for every good work. You are able to look after your own life and those around you. God's blessings come in an abundance that supplies more than "enough."

The authors of Scripture gave many biblical examples of God's abundance. For example:

✓ The story from John 6:5–13 (which was previously discussed) where the little boy gave his lunch to

Jesus. The multitudes were fed until they were full. There was so much abundance in the provision that the leftovers filled twelve baskets.

✓ In 1 Kings 17:10–16, when the widow baked her last handful of flour and gave it to the prophet Elijah, the miracle of a barrelful of inexhaustible flour occurred in her life. This woman was starving. Yet, the bold prophet told her to use her last remaining flour to make him a cake. He had walked so long and so close with God that asking for a widow's last meal was no big thing. He had experienced firsthand God's miracles. He knew that her trusting God's prophet and doing what he requested was the key to her miracle.

✓ In 2 Kings 4:1–7, the widow approached the prophet Elisha because the creditor was claiming her two boys as settlement for her late husband's debts. The prophet asked her what she had. She replied that she had only a small bottle of oil. He then told her to pour out the oil into pots. She borrowed pots from everyone in the village. She poured and poured. Finally, every pot was filled and there were no more left empty. The oil didn't stop flowing until she stopped pouring!

In these accounts, each person first gave, and then he or she discovered the power of God as He released the miracle.

Obedience Does Not Equal Poverty

God *never* said that getting right with Him will result in poverty. It is difficult to find anyone in Scripture whom God blessed who did not enjoy prosperity in his life.

Prosperity comes because certain principles are being observed. The primary principle in action, as taught through the authors of Scripture, is that these people honored God with their tithes and offerings.

———◆———

This will probably shock many, but the Bible was written by extraordinarily successful and wealthy people. Here are just a few biblical examples of patriarchs who honored God and then were richly blessed:

1. **Abraham**:

He was considered the father of tithing. He tithed to a priest named Melchizedek:

> *Then Melchizedek king of Salem brought out bread and wine; he was the priest of God Most High. And he blessed him and said: "Blessed be Abram of God Most High, Possessor of heaven and earth; and blessed be God Most High, Who has delivered your enemies into your hand." And he gave him a tithe of all.*
>
> (Genesis 14:18–20)

Romans 4:12 instructs us to walk in the steps of the faith of Abraham. Melchizedek is considered by many scholars to be a pre-incarnate appearance of Jesus Himself. At the very least, Jesus is presented as being of the same order and nature as this great and mysterious priest.

> *As He also says in another place: You are a priest forever according to the order of Melchizedek....where the forerunner has entered for us, even Jesus, having become High Priest forever according to the order of Melchizedek....Now consider how great this man was,*

to whom even the patriarch Abraham gave a tenth of the spoils. (Hebrews 5:6; 6:20; 7:4)

Thus, it can be said that Abraham, one of the wealthiest men in his time, tithed to Christ—and that was at least four hundred years before the Old Testament and the laws of Moses were written!

2. **Jacob**:

And this stone which I have set as a pillar shall be God's house, and of all that You give me I will surely give a tenth to You....Thus the man became exceedingly prosperous, and had large flocks, female and male servants, and camels and donkeys.
(Genesis 28:22; 30:43)

3. **Isaac**:

Then Isaac sowed in that land, and reaped in the same year a hundredfold; and the LORD blessed him. The man began to prosper, and continued prospering until he became very prosperous; for he had possessions of flocks and possessions of herds and a great number of servants. So the Philistines envied him.
(Genesis 26:12–14)

4. **Jesus**:

Jesus was treated as a king from the time He was born and throughout His ministry.

During the three years of Jesus' ministry, wealthy women who followed Him provided for Him.

And Joanna the wife of Chuza, Herod's steward, and Susanna, and many others who provided for Him from their substance. (Luke 8:3)

These people were wealthy, and there were many of them. They provided for all of the Messiah's needs. The group traveling with Christ received so much that they needed a treasurer to keep track of it all (Judas). Even Jesus Himself had direct access to large sums of money and valuables.

From early antiquity, when kings visited other kings, it was a diplomatic expectation for them to bring extravagant gifts to the king they were visiting, whether a child king or an adult. At his birth, Jesus received gold, frankincense, and myrrh from several kings. Despite tradition, the number of the Magi who visited Jesus was not necessarily three. (This idea is based on the fact that there were three gifts mentioned.) There were probably many more than three.

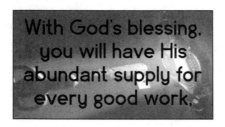

With God's blessing, you will have His abundant supply for every good work.

Nor were the gifts three single items of gold, frankincense, and myrrh. Rather, these were probably the headings of inventories under which many different items would have been included, which was the normal practice for recording indexes of gifts presented to kings. The wealth and influence of the Magi is clearly considerable because of the impact their coming had upon Herod. The gifts were for Jesus personally, not for His family. Yet it would be reasonable to presume that once He understood what His wealth was, He would have shared it with them.

Texts from as far back as 1850 BC record the vast inventories of gifts that were exchanged between kings of greater or lesser degrees when they met with each other.

They reveal prodigious quantities of gold, ebony, ivory, lapis lazuli, garments, and sweet oil being sent in each direction as part of diplomatic protocol. Even though the value of these gifts adds up to incredible amounts, they pale when compared to first millennium BC practices.

In 889 BC, Osorkon gave gifts to Egypt totaling 445 metric tons of gold (nearly $350 million dollars in today's rate of exchange) in the form of vessels, statues, furnishings, and the like. Gifts of an extraordinary abundance came with the Queen of Sheba to the court of Solomon. But we are told that her breath was taken away at the grandeur of Solomon's vast wealth.

An abundance of records detail what was considered diplomatically acceptable in the amounts of gift giving. In fact, if a king's wealth was not represented in his gift, or if the stature of the receiving king was not sufficiently reflected, the receiving king would let the giver understand in no uncertain terms that he had been slighted by the meanness of the gift.

5. **Paul**:

He traveled three times around the world, had enough to pay for a Roman trial, supported all those who traveled with him (Acts 20:34), and was kept in prison for two years by Felix, the Roman procurator of Judea, for the sole reason that Felix *hoped to obtain a bribe from the apostle* (Acts 24:26). Felix would not have waited so long for just a trivial amount; he knew Paul was capable of paying a substantial sum, and he was prepared to wait.

Paul, a strict Pharisee, would have observed tithing as a regular practice all his life. He encouraged generous giving and taught people to lay aside at the beginning of each week the firstfruits of their increase.

On the first day of the week let each one of you lay something aside, storing up as he may prosper.
(1 Corinthians 16:2)

After listening to ministers in many churches, we could be forgiven for imagining that the writers of the Bible were a bundle of poor hermits living on handouts, dwelling on the deepest issues of life, and committing their thoughts solely to Scripture. That couldn't be further from the truth.

6. **Moses**:

Moses wrote the first five books of the Bible, was raised as a prince in Egypt, then lived as a shepherd, and eventually was set in place by God as the leader of all of Israel.

Though he led a nation of slaves, Moses was no pauper. God provided great riches for the Israelites in a miraculous way: He caused the Egyptians to give them all of their gold and silver—a financial devastation from which Egypt has not recovered to this day.

Now the children of Israel had done according to the word of Moses, and they had asked from the Egyptians articles of silver, articles of gold, and clothing. And the LORD had given the people favor in the sight of the Egyptians, so that they granted them what they requested. Thus they plundered the Egyptians.
(Exodus 12:35–36)

Furthermore, Moses had been legendary as a military leader in Egypt. He was the man who wrote how the world was created. He revealed the truth about the fall of man and God's promised redemption. He explained the flood, the beginning of the various races, the birthing of the nation of Israel, the life of Abraham. He related his experience with God on Sinai and the laws for living that came from that. It was by God's own design that a successful, wealthy man penned the origins of our entire world!

7. **Job**:

Job was considered the wealthiest man in the East—the "Bill Gates" of his day.

Also, his possessions were seven thousand sheep, three thousand camels, five hundred yoke of oxen, five hundred female donkeys, and a very large household, so that this man was the greatest of all the people of the East. (Job 1:3)

Job presented offerings to God regularly:

He would rise early in the morning and offer burnt offerings....Thus Job did regularly. (Job 1:5)

Job tackled one of the most perplexing and difficult questions that had plagued man for centuries: "Why is there pain in the world?" He suffered some of the worst calamities anyone could, yet his integrity toward God remained firm. God was so sure of Job's faithfulness that He allowed Satan to destroy all his possessions, kill all his children, then destroy his health to the point where Job despised living! Yet, he remained true to God, even when his wife urged him to curse God, and his friends accused him of hidden sinfulness and pride. Everything that could go wrong did go wrong—and then his friends attacked him when he was down! After his trial, which took about nine months, the Lord reversed Job's circumstances. He became twice as wealthy as before, had seven sons and three of the most beautiful daughters, and the Lord told his friends to ask Job to pray for them (Job 42:7–16).

God's kingdom greatly benefits from having leaders who are enormously successful.

God had wanted to bless this man with twice as much as He had, but He also knew He could trust Job to remain true under the worst of conditions and write something that would comfort people in every generation. All this was written by the wealthiest man of his day, in a book generally acknowledged by Bible scholars as the first book in the entire Bible to be written.

8. **David**:

God referred to David as *"a man after My own heart"* (1 Samuel 13:14). *After* God chose him to be king over Israel, he became a *billionaire* and gave today's equivalent of two and a half billion dollars of his personal fortune to the building fund for the temple of God.

> *Besides, in my devotion to the temple of my God I now give my personal treasures of gold and silver for the temple of my God, over and above everything I have provided for this holy temple.*
>
> (1 Chronicles 29:3)

It is not a poor man who can give that kind of gift for a building fund! Yet this is the same David who wrote the beautiful psalms of praise we sing all around the world today.

This same David wrote psalms of brokenness and contrition, psalms of crying out to God in anguish, psalms of prophecy about Jesus Christ, psalms of instruction from the Word of God, psalms of passion for God Himself—psalms of a *billionaire*.

Twenty-two times David referred to the offerings he brought into the house of God—his tithing and fulfillment of the pledges he had made to the Lord.

9. **Solomon**:

Solomon was even wealthier than his father David. The Queen of Sheba visited him and was rendered breathless by the sheer magnificence of all she saw—and she was no beggar queen by any means. First Kings 10:10 tells us that she gave Solomon extravagant gifts; her gift of gold alone was worth around $4 million dollars at today's rate of exchange.

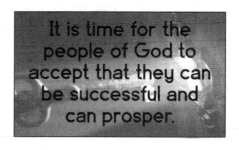

It is time for the people of God to accept that they can be successful and can prosper.

Solomon exceeded all the kings of other surrounding nations in wealth. Yet this is the same Solomon who revealed the secrets to life in the book of Proverbs, the deep sayings of Ecclesiastes, and the passions of tested love in the romance of Song of Songs.

Every day around the world people shape their lives by the wisdom found in Proverbs. These holy Scriptures were not recorded by a poor man, but by the wealthiest king of his era.

10. **The Prophets**:

Even the prophets were not considered poor. Isaiah came from a wealthy background. Jonah had enough money to purchase a ticket on a boat to a distant country, and Jeremiah was able to go out and buy acreage for seventeen shekels (about $9,000—one shekel equaled four days' wages) when the Lord told him to (Jeremiah 32:9).

Preachers Are Not Exempt from Financial Blessings

Some people imagine that if they fail in the world, then it must be a sign they are meant to be in the ministry. What a bankrupt thought! The kingdom of God greatly benefits from having among its top leaders God-fearing people who are enormously successful. Poverty and failure are not qualifications to become preachers, pastors, and ministers, who must be great givers themselves in order to be as successful as possible so they can lead others into the same way of living.

The witness of preachers is made more forcible when they have resources and wealth at their disposal to bless people in this world. Simply spouting out truths from the pulpit and saying, "Well, bless you," to those in need is not quite enough. They need to prove that what they preach improves people's lives, including their own.

The poor man's wisdom is despised, and his words are not heard.   (Ecclesiastes 9:16)

The church has not been listened to in the commercial, financial, entertainment, and sporting worlds, not only because we have practically retreated from those areas, but also because we seem to have practically shunned success in those areas. Then we complain when the secular "stars" promote values that conflict with the spiritual and moral health of the nation. But if the church counted among its Christ-loving followers the highest earners, the most successful people, and the best in the world, then we would find people paying far more serious attention to what we say, because of our obvious

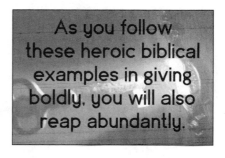

As you follow these heroic biblical examples in giving boldly, you will also reap abundantly.

success. That may not sound like the proper response to wealth, but it's just the way the world thinks. The tragedy is that we have to convince people of a message that appears to minimize people, not maximize them. To the world, the Christian message appears to seriously handicap people for a successful life rather than release them into a fully developed, wonderful existence on this earth.

It is high time for the people of God to accept that they *can* be successful, they *can* prosper, and that such success will be a compelling message to the world *and* will finance all the things we want to accomplish for God's purposes.

One of the surest ways to succeed at something is to spend time with a person who has done just that. Those who spend copious amounts of time embracing the tenets and teachings of Scripture are going to inherit the same spirit and principles of success and abundance that accompanied the lives of the wealthy and accomplished men who wrote it.

If you want every pot filled and nothing left empty, then follow the bold examples of giving set by the authors of the Bible, and you *will* reap abundantly!

KEY #8

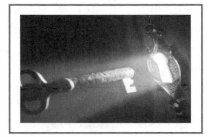

PROSPERITY:
THE WILL OF GOD

Beloved, I pray that you may prosper in all things
and be in health, just as your soul prospers.
—3 John 1:2

P eople all over the world want to prosper. It's not an
abnormal or negative desire. Governments want
their countries and their people to prosper. Fathers
want their families to prosper. Husbands and wives want
their marriages to prosper. Business people want their
businesses to prosper. Employees want to prosper in their
jobs.

To prosper is to do well in every area of your life and
achieve your goals. Not only do we all want to prosper in
what we do, but God also wants us to prosper. Prosperity
is the will of God—it is He who is at work to make you succeed in this life.

We could easily imagine that the aged apostle John would pray for great spirituality as his number one desire for his congregation. Yet, at the end of his incredible ministry, the great man of God prays simply for his friends to prosper and to have success, to achieve their dreams and do well in their life's journey.

It is incredible that many Christians balk at that concept. Throughout history, some have even *vowed* to be poor, thinking that deliberate poverty somehow pleases God. Certainly it is vital that the material things of the world do not displace God as first in our lives. Everything should orbit around God and be surrendered in service to Him. However, because of some Dark Ages aesthetic, poverty somehow became enshrined as a godly virtue. That same thinking appeals today to some Christians who want to please God through their own human efforts.

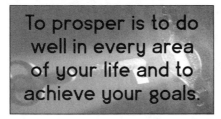

To prosper is to do well in every area of your life and to achieve your goals.

In light of the excesses of the church in Rome at that time, and the corruption of the leaders of the church in an age where money and power combined to pervert God's purposes for the church, it is understandable that a stand for Christ should include renouncing wealth. But that was never the stance of Scripture. It was *the devil himself* who managed to establish poverty as a deeply held belief in the church! The enemy's assault on truth has successfully hampered the church in later centuries from accomplishing many things it has been called to.

However, Paul warned us not to be cheated out of our reward through humility parading as piety:

Let no one cheat you of your reward, taking delight in false humility. (Colossians 2:18)

The word *humility* is taken from a combination of two Greek words: *tapeinophrosune*, which means "depressed, humiliated in circumstances or disposition, not joyful but base, cast down, humble, of low degree and estate," and *phren*, meaning "to rein in or curb the midriff (as a partition of the body)." Figuratively speaking, humility means "reining in the feelings, the heart, the mind (by extension), and the understanding (our cognitive abilities)."

Some people promote "the reigning in" of feelings and mind as pleasing to God. Yet, it is actually a religious spirit that cheats us out of our inheritance in Christ. The church has been notorious for justifying small, poor, backward thinking as being "for the Lord," as if when we do things small and second-rate, we're doing it for God! That is ridiculous. God wants us to think bigger than we ever have before in our lives. We are not to limit God with our limited mindsets, but to release Him with ever-bigger thinking, dreaming, and accomplishing great exploits for Him.

Humility, Not Servility

We are called to humility, not to a servility that embraces poverty and depression as though they were a form of piety that pleases the Father.

If poverty really were the will of God for us, then to fully do the will of God would mean to ensure that we live in a perpetual state of utter poverty—which means no living in countries where the government looks after the poor because that would violate one's poverty status. True poverty would require taking up residence on the streets of a city like Calcutta, scavenging for food, and begging on the streets. Now *that* would be real poverty. And we definitely couldn't allow ourselves to be educated because that's a way to improve our lives—we might even accidentally prosper and really upset God!

If that scenario is overreactive hyperbole, then what do people mean when they say they don't believe Christians should be rich or have abundance? The answer is usually that "Christians should have *just enough*." Just enough for whom? Just enough for your family to get by on? That would have to be about the most selfish kind of "Christianity" possible! It's expensive being a true Christian. To be the good Samaritan, one cannot be poor or cheap.

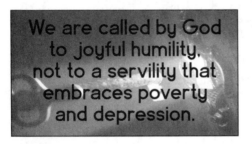

We are called by God to joyful humility, not to a servility that embraces poverty and depression.

By Jesus' own definition, being someone's neighbor means being able to pick them up when they're half dead, take them to the hospital, and have them cared for until they are healed and well again. Believers should have enough wealth to be able to carry out at least that much. What good is a Christian who sees someone in need but can't respond because he's lived by a poverty mind-set, so all he can do is say, "Well, I'll pray for you, brother"? We should be able to pay our neighbor's rent if he loses his job. We should be able to give a single mother a car if she needs one. We can't fight the enemy effectively if we deny ourselves the money that it costs to win many of life's battles. That is why the Lord *wants* to give us an overflowing abundance! He loves us and wants us to be His witnesses to this generation.

God's Will Is That We Succeed at His Purpose

And you shall remember the LORD your God, for it is
He who gives you power to get wealth, that He may es-
tablish His covenant which He swore to your fathers,
as it is this day.   (Deuteronomy 8:18)

God is not raising an army to be defeated! He does not give birth to people so they will fail in life. It is not only God's will, but also His *great pleasure* for His children to prosper in this life.

Both the Old and New Testaments reveal that *giving* is a major key to prosperity.

The generous soul will be made rich, and he who
waters will also be watered himself....He who has a
generous eye will be blessed, for he gives of his bread
to the poor.   (Proverbs 11:25; 22:9)

According to a 1997 article in *Fortune* magazine, the top twenty-five philanthropists in the U.S. gave away more than $1.5 billion in 1996. The most generous was George Soros, president of Soros Fund Management, who donated $350 million. Of those top twenty-five philanthropists, only four had inherited fortunes. Most attributed their generosity in part to religious backgrounds, and most were givers even before they became wealthy. *Generosity* is a key principle to a great life, even for people who don't acknowledge God.

In 1992 the following article about a generous man appeared in a Sydney newspaper:

Eric Storm Tells How to Be a Millionaire: "You just give it away"

by Peter Lalor

Eric Storm admits he is a most unusual multi-millionaire.

In a cluttered north shore kitchen, with only a bar radiator and a tartan rug to fight off the winter chill, the 103-year-old sits on a plastic chair at a small card table and plays the stock market. With the television blaring in the middle of the room, an old adding machine, a pile of business papers and a telephone, he has built up a $17 million fortune after starting with $800,000.

He owns a modest cottage, a second-hand car, exists on a frugal diet of salads and millet linseed porridge, never eats at restaurants, and has no interest in money apart from when he makes it or gives it away. To date, Mr. Storm has made over 11,000 donations, totaling $27 million, to charity groups. Every cent he makes or controls is earmarked for the same fate.

On Monday, his tireless and selfless commitment was rewarded when Mr. Storm was awarded a Member of the Order of Australia medal.

The stock market player says he was honored by the recognition. Still, it is not going to make much change to the lifestyle of the man who retired in 1930 after making a fortune trading in the Dutch East Indies.

Returning to Australia, Mr. Storm played the market full time and built up a fortune for himself and lifetime friend, Fred Archer.

"We started to make money, and then we wondered what to do with it," he said yesterday. "Mr. Archer was a very simple living man, so we decided to give it away. What else can you do with it?"

When the obvious suggestions are made, Mr. Storm is gruff in his dismissal. "Is a big house going to give me pleasure?" he says. "Is a Rolls Royce and going to restaurants going to make me happy? I'd be dead in a fortnight eating all that muck. I live simply. This house is comfortable, all that I want. What would I want any more for? I don't want a great house mansion and half a dozen servants or to drive a big car and show the world that I've got a checkbook around my neck. For 30 odd years we never told anyone. It was only at my 100th birthday that my other [charity fund] directors insisted I tell what I was doing. I'm not very interested in material things."

Mr. Storm distributes the profits through the Fred Archer Charitable Trust, at the rate of $500,000 a year. In the warmer months, he visits the institutions that receive part of the dividend.

A fellow director, Don Logan, said the old man was extremely sharp. "He does all the trading and makes all the decisions," he said. "He is on the phone to the broker every day."

Mr. Storm has been a strict vegetarian since getting ill 70 years ago. He believes he continues to make money because he has no interest in it. "I believe in giving and helping people," he said. "I think one of the reasons I keep making money is because I give it away. It's some divine power, or something, which gives me the ability to pick the right shares."

The Pleasure of God

Let them shout for joy and be glad, who favor my righteous cause; and let them say continually, "Let the LORD be magnified, who has pleasure in the prosperity of His servant." (Psalm 35:27)

If there's one thing that God gets a kick out of, if there's one thing that makes God smile, it is when His kids do well and prosper. God takes pleasure in the prosperity of His servants! He gets great joy out of the success of His beloved children. He gets a kick out of our prosperity! He is not happy when we lose or fail; His joy is in our *success*.

God doesn't give up on us, either—even when we fail once or twice. No father is going to give up on his child when she is just beginning to walk. If the child falls two or three times, the father doesn't say, "Well, you had your chance. You're never going to walk, so don't ever try it again."

Unintentional failure is a building block of growth. It's an understood fact that learning to do anything involves failure every now and then. We are meant to learn from the experience and get up and try again. Never quitting is the foundation of great success.

God Makes It Happen

The ability to create wealth is a gift from God. This ability has generosity as its basic element. People with the gift of giving also tend to have a gift for generating money. Whatever they touch seems to be successful. As these people give, they receive—ideas, inventions, strategies, contacts, opportunities, openings, perfect timings—all coming from the hand of God to help them become successful. The purpose of this prosperity is to establish the covenant of God on the earth. Preaching the gospel, building churches, paying ministers and supporting the work of God all require vast funding.

The enormous end-time harvest will call for all the prosperity the church can generate.

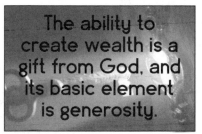

The ability to create wealth is a gift from God, and its basic element is generosity.

I firmly believe that it is God's purpose to raise an army of financiers for His kingdom. As God grants us the ability to make wealth, we will find ourselves engaged in all sorts of adventures effective in creating enormous finances for God!

KEY #9

THE PACE OF PROSPERITY

A faithful man will abound with blessings, but he who hastens to be rich will not go unpunished.
—Proverbs 28:20

P rosperity does not come in a hurry. In fact, Proverbs tells us that riches gained quickly *"will not be blessed at the end"* (Proverbs 20:21) and will *"fly away"* (23:5).

Wealth comes in stages. That is a law of life. Seeds become trees. Small beginnings travel through stages of growth to become large successes.

We delude ourselves if we think our prosperity will come in a flash. When our family was young, we bought a small yacht to sail the waterways of Sydney, where we lived. The boat was nineteen feet long, our children were small, and we had a blast on that boat. In fact, we spent one stretch of ten days on that little boat with five of us onboard! It was fantastic. But then our children grew. We needed more room, so we bought a larger, secondhand boat. It was thirty-three feet long and cost at least ten times more than the previous one. Later we sold that and purchased our next boat, which was forty feet long. It cost five times what the last boat cost. This was the boat we dreamed of owning eighteen years ago. With a little patience, progressing step by step, we eventually got there.

We gave our first boat to our building fund as the sacrifice component for building our church. We didn't have a boat after that for five years. Then one day my wife and I were sitting on a wharf sipping coffee and looking at the moored yachts. We decided we would go and buy the second boat. We could have said, "Oh, we'll just wait until the Lord 'gives' us our next boat," because we had "given" (sown) our first one to Him. But God doesn't move until we do; so we stepped out to purchase that boat. We found one we liked, arranged a loan, and paid it off over the next couple of years. The incredible times we had with our family and friends on that boat bonded us forever.

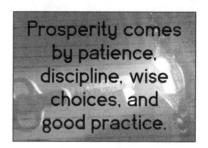

Prosperity comes by patience, discipline, wise choices, and good practice.

God's provision comes mostly though very normal means. It is not unusual to experience extraordinary supernatural supply from God, but He usually works through normal means.

Prosperity comes in steps. Many of the principles by which we gain ground are the same as those by which we maintain that ground. The prosperity that comes by patience, discipline, wise choices, and good practice, will be maintained by those same principles. However, those who rush to become prosperous quickly and easily haven't learned the ways of prospering and will experience difficulty holding on to their blessings for long.

KEY #10

MAINTAINING PROSPERITY

*Will you set your eyes on that which is not? For riches
certainly make themselves wings; they fly away like
an eagle toward heaven.*
—Proverbs 23:5

Money is powerful. Its attraction is undeniable. However, keep in mind that the Christian's prosperity comes from God. If we place our focus on money rather than on God, then our money will *"fly away."*

A major idol of our modern world is money. People trust in money, work for it, sacrifice health and family for it, even sacrifice their integrity for it, all in the false thinking that money will deliver them and give them a life of blessing. But the life we all dream for comes not from this "god of money," it comes only from the one true God, the Lord of heaven and earth. That is why giving money is so powerful. Every time we give money to God, we establish the fact that money does not rule us, we rule it. Every time we give, we declare that

God is our God, not money. We are surrendering money into His hands. We are making money serve us, and not allowing it to rule over us. When we give, we are establishing the lordship of Christ and the servanthood of money.

The generosity of our giving establishes the faith we have in our God to supply what we have given. If we give in ways that leave our finances unaffected, then we remain "safe." However, when we give so that we are left with need, then we are taking true steps of faith in God, who has promised to supply all of our needs (Philippians 4:19).

But seek first the kingdom of God and His righteousness, and all these things shall be added to you.
(Matthew 6:33)

Even though God promises us prosperity, our vision is not to be money itself. According to Matthew 6:33, if we seek the kingdom first, then all "these things" that we would like will be "added" to us. The more money we have, the more things we will have that have the potential to consume it. Ecclesiastes 5:11 says that the more you have, the more people come to help you spend it.

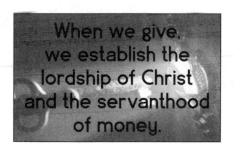
When we give, we establish the lordship of Christ and the servanthood of money.

A major factor in maintaining wealth is remaining focused on what *produces it*, rather than on the wealth itself.

A lawyer friend of mine told me how his business was nearly destroyed because he had ignored the bread and butter of his business and focused on the high-risk cases that had the potential for bringing in big money. Those cases were rare, but exciting. He ignored keeping good relationships with the real estate agents who referred clients to him when they purchased homes. He forgot how important the basics were, and he suffered for it. Maintaining wealth is always about looking after the basics, staying on track, and *keeping the main thing the main thing!*

PRINCIPLES OF TITHING

KEY #11

TITHING

"Bring all the tithes into the storehouse, that there may be food in My house, and try Me now in this," says the Lord of hosts, "If I will not open for you the windows of heaven and pour out for you such blessing that there will not be room enough to receive it."
—Malachi 3:10

As the Scripture above indicates, giving the tithe is directly associated with "opening the windows of heaven." This opening is what releases the blessings of God—His abundant provision—upon His people.

If God says that when the tithe is brought into His house He will open the windows of heaven, then the implication is that the windows of heaven were *closed* prior to that point. The only other times the phrase *"windows of heaven"* appears in Scripture are in Genesis 7:11 and 8:2, in reference to the great flood. Part of the cause of the flood was that

God "opened the windows of heaven." That phrase refers to a great outpouring of rain on the earth. For the crop farming community of Israel, rain was one of the greatest blessings they could receive. Their entire livelihood hinged on whether or not it would rain.

On the other hand, judgment often came in the form of drought (Haggai 1:11; 2 Chronicles 7:13). The weather is something that farmers have no control over. They can plough the fields and sow the seed, but when it comes to weather conditions, a farmer is completely at the mercy of the weather—which means at the mercy of *God*.

No matter what field of business we are in, we all depend on some things that are simply beyond our control. The real estate market, the stock market, government policies, economic trends, market trends, can all turn up or down, for us or against us. The opening of the *"windows of heaven"* refers to those situations that we have no control over— "windows" that are closed or opened in accordance with God's will alone.

God says He will arrange favorable circumstances for us in certain areas if we are faithful in bringing the tithe into the storehouse. When we honor God with our tithe, surprising coincidences, providential meetings with key people, favor with those who have influence—all sorts of unforeseen things can come into play on our behalf. After all, *"Bring all the tithes"* is not a suggestion, it's a *command*—but one that, if we obey it, comes with a promise of blessings!

Our Attitude Toward Tithing

> *"What a weariness this is," you say, and you sniff at me, says the LORD of hosts.* (Malachi 1:13 NRSV)

Malachi rebuked the people for their sneering, weary attitude toward the tithes and offerings. Yet, giving to God is one of the highest callings we have—one that can mightily expand our tent pegs.

During my services, before we receive the offering, I usually preach for about five to ten minutes on the topic of giving. I make no apologies about that. Sadly, I have found that people who have a problem with that are generally Christians, and not the unchurched. Nearly every year during the month of June I preach about money, prosperity, and giving. The amazing thing is that our records and graphs show that—apart from Christmas and Easter when we host major outreaches—we see the largest number of people coming to Christ in our services during June.

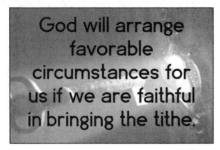

God will arrange favorable circumstances for us if we are faithful in bringing the tithe.

Not long ago, a pastor in our movement felt that God was calling him to leave his church and begin traveling. But he also felt he should still base himself in our church, so for the first year he was often in our services. One Sunday in June, as I preached on the topic of tithing, before we took the offering, he began to think, "Phil...give it a rest." He had found himself wondering why I addressed the issue of tithing in every single service. An *attitude* had developed within him, he later told me. Then one day as he was listening to me preach, he said something "clicked" inside of him about giving—the light went on! He had never before enjoyed any great prosperity, but faith that it could happen began to well up within him.

Since that time, his income through his ministry has increased tenfold. He also found that when he went to minister at other venues, the income of the church he ministered in increased because he *imparted a revelation* about giving that personally applied to him. As a result, many other doors have since opened up. Even though finances are not this preacher's primary ministry, it has become a powerful new arrow in his quiver. At the point when he had grown weary of offering, God grabbed his heart and turned him around.

> *Do not forget my teaching, but keep my commands in your heart, for they will prolong your life many years* ***and bring you prosperity.***
> (Proverbs 3:1–2 NIV, emphasis added)

KEY #12

THE CURSE OF
NOT TITHING

*You are cursed with a curse, for you have robbed
Me, even this whole nation.*
—Malachi 3:9

P roverbs 26:2 declares that a curse without a cause cannot land. However, if there is a cause, the curse can land
and will do its damage. Blessings can impact a person's
life in very real and powerful ways, just as curses can.

Throughout Scripture, both blessings and curses are
promised as a result of the choices we make during our lives.
The most graphic example of this was on the dawn of Israel's
invasion of Canaan. For centuries, God had promised the
Canaan land to the Hebrews. After their deliverance from
Egypt and wandering through the desert for forty years, they
were finally about to enter their Promised Land. The first
city the Israelites had to overwhelm was the great walled

city of Jericho—a task for which they were completely inadequate. However, through a strategy given to them by God, the Israelites destroyed Jericho's defenses entirely and swept to victory.

But God had given them strict instructions that *everything* in Jericho was to be destroyed. Only the silver and gold and the vessels of bronze and iron were to be spared and put into the treasury of the house of the Lord. Other than that, the entire city was devoted to destruction, to be the firstfruits of the Israelites' Promised Land—the *tithe* into the future prosperity that was going to come upon them. But temptation got the better of one man, Achan, who took from among the spoils *"a beau-*

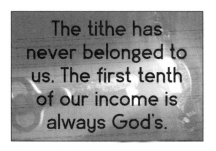

The tithe has never belonged to us. The first tenth of our income is always God's.

tiful Babylonian garment, two hundred shekels of silver, and a wedge of gold weighing fifty shekels" (Joshua 7:21) and buried them in the dirt beneath his tent.

Hot in the flush of victory, Joshua was quick to survey the next target to be conquered: Ai, a small, unwalled city of 3,000. He sent only a small troop on the mission and never bothered to seek God as he had done at Jericho. Thus, he had no strategy from the Lord. Not surprisingly, the mission failed and thirty-six men were killed. When they returned from the battle, humiliated and defeated, Joshua fell on his face in desperation and asked God why. Almighty Jehovah answered by accusing Israel of sin. Joshua was mystified and asked how that could be. The Lord declared that someone had taken spoils that were to have been devoted to Him. By the casting of the lot, Achan was revealed as the guilty party, and the Israelites stoned, burned, and then buried him and his family under a pile of rocks!

God then spoke to Joshua and gave him a new strategy for the taking of Ai. The Israelite army followed the plan and was successful. They continued on with a refreshed reverence for God, with Joshua having learned how urgent it is to give God the firstfruits in order to enjoy victory.

If you were to enter my house and steal my stereo, refrigerator, television, car, and clothes and then come to me the next day and ask me to bless you with a gift, the chances of you receiving what you asked for would be slim indeed! Yet, that is exactly the picture God gives us of those who withhold the tithe. He declares that they have stolen from Him by withholding money that belongs to Him.

The Message of Jericho

The tithe has never belonged to us. The first tenth of our income is always God's. As mature Christians, it should be unthinkable to hold our hand out for a blessing from God, when we have His property in our other hand.

The message of Jericho is clear: When we fail to obey God with regard to the tithe, we invite a curse into our lives—a curse that could bring with it the loss of many good things. If money that belongs to God is sitting in your bank account, the curse on that money will travel into the entire account, and it could very well dwindle away. If money that belongs to God has instead gone back into your business, then your business is in jeopardy.

However, if the tithe is brought to the house of God and given to the Lord, then it becomes a blessing. Wherever the tithe originates from—the bank account, the business, the profit from a sale, a gift—blessing will come upon that area.

The blessing of God is a very powerful thing. Our obedience to His Word brings about a big return. Disobedience, on the other hand, puts in an effort that receives little return. Under God's blessing, every dollar goes twice as far. Under a curse, it seems the money goes nowhere. It's all spent, and we have little to show for it.

There is never neutral ground with God. It's heaven or hell, light or darkness, blessing or curse. When we hold onto money that belongs to the Lord, we are holding on to a curse. When we are tithing that money to the Lord by bringing it into His house, we are gaining enormous blessing over our lives.

The Jericho story also reveals that our responsibility to tithe is both individual and corporate. The sin of Achan caused the entire nation to suffer defeat. If God's people in every country around the world would begin bringing the whole tithe into the house of God every Sunday, we would see blessings fall upon the church in ways unprecedented in church history. The harvest of souls, the growth of the church, and the unity of the believers would be increased beyond our wildest dreams almost overnight. We must urge the saints everywhere to tithe, simply so that the great blessings of God will fall upon the church in God-sized ways!

Honor the LORD with your wealth, with the firstfruits of all your crops; then your barns will be filled to overflowing, and your vats will brim over with new wine. (Proverbs 3:9–10 NIV)

KEY #13

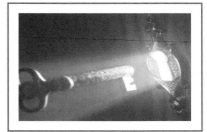

THE BLESSINGS OF TITHING: THE WINDOWS OF HEAVEN

That there may be food in My house.
—Malachi 3:10

Some people aren't getting anything out of church anymore. They're leaving the church because they're not being fed. Sometimes, when I'm visiting other churches, people tell me they are going to leave because the pastor doesn't "bring the food of the Word." I find that, all too often, the problem is simply that these people have ceased tithing. Perhaps someone told them they didn't think the church was spending its money properly. Maybe they didn't like the spending levels shown in the church's annual report. Or possibly they had been experiencing problems with their own cash flow and decided to stop tithing until things improved. Gradually, however, they feel a decrease of spiritual food coming to them in the church. They become critical and judgmental of nearly everything around them.

Then, their hearts close off to the ministry God has given them, and they begin a spiritual withering.

That begins the vicious cycle: they claim they are not being fed by the ministry that feeds them, so they fail to give to the ministry. Then, the more they withhold God's tithe, the less they feel fed from their church; and the less they feel fed, the more they withhold—and they never receive God's blessings. If they will simply take a step of faith and do what God tells them concerning the tithe, then they will see His blessings—even to the point of feeling well fed at their church.

The simplest of messages can contain the deepest of truths if we are open and eager to hear. Yet there is another principle at work at the same time: if people are tithers, then it is a law of Scripture that he **will** *receive food in the house of God!*

Let God Prove It

When it comes to tithing, God challenges us to put Him to the test:

> *"Bring all the tithes into the storehouse, that there may be food in My house, and try Me now in this,"* says the LORD of hosts, "If I will not open for you the windows of heaven and pour out for you such blessing that there will not be room enough to receive it."*
> (Malachi 3:10)

This is the only invitation in the entire Bible in which God challenges us to put Him to the test!

✓ *The Living Bible* says, *"Try it! Let Me prove it to you!"*

— 71 —

✓ The KJV says, *"And prove Me now herewith."*

✓ The NIV says, *"Test Me in this."*

✓ The NRSV says, *"Put Me to the test."*

✓ The NKJV says, *"Try Me now in this."*

God says that if we bring all the tithes into the church, two things will happen:

1. **There will be food in His house**. Spiritual nourishment is in the house of God when the people are tithing.

2. **He will pour out such blessing on you** that there will not be room enough for you to contain it. You will be unable to accommodate the blessing of God when He pours it out on you!

Awhile ago, a middle-aged legal firm manager and his family became Christians and came to our church. After awhile, they decided to become members. When he was confronted with the issue of tithing, he felt very uncomfortable with the idea. One of our pastors counseled him and suggested that he try it just for ninety days, and if at the end of that time he experienced no tangible benefits, he should go ahead and stop tithing. This seemed fair enough to the man, and he started tithing. Almost immediately he received a hefty promotion from his firm, a brand new car, a raise in salary, and other blessings so that he could not help but relate the success to the fact that he had begun to tithe.

It bears repeating:

[I will] *open for you the windows of heaven and pour out for you such blessing that there will not be room enough to receive it.* (Malachi 3:10)

KEY #14

THE TITHE: TO WHERE?

You shall keep the Feast of Unleavened Bread...none shall appear before Me empty [handed].
—Exodus 23:15

The tithe belongs *in the house of God.* That is not a metaphor; it refers to nothing other than *the local church.*

The Scripture tells us to bring our tithe, which means we don't send our tithe, we ourselves turn up at church *with it!* God wants us gathered with believers in order to worship, to fellowship, to be held accountable to one another, and to minister to Him and to each other.

The other major part of the purpose of gathering together in the church body includes bringing the tithe. When we go to church services, we have a purpose beyond simply showing up. In Exodus 23:15, the word *empty* means "in vain." We are meant to appear before God with a full hand, ready to give; not arriving in vain, or empty-handed. Our purpose in coming is not ethereal, it's tangible. We haven't come just to receive from God; we've also come *to give back to God* from among what He has blessed us with.

The tithe also releases the ministry to bring the Word at a level of revelation that feeds the people of God. For example, it's a physical, natural law of life that you pay for the food you eat. It is not advisable to eat in a restaurant and leave without paying—no matter what reason you give, doing a dine and dash won't fly! You may say you're eager to help the restaurant down the road that is struggling, so you're not going to pay the one you've just eaten at. Or you could try the excuse that you don't believe in paying for food since you never asked to be born in the first place. Or you might tell the chef you didn't like what was dished up or that the maitre d' treated you like a leper or you didn't like the color of your food or the pattern on the wallpaper, but none of those excuses will work. *You eat, you pay!* Those are the rules.

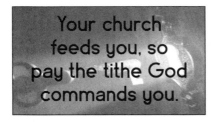
Your church feeds you, so pay the tithe God commands you.

Same thing in the church: your church feeds you, so pay the tithe that God commands you.

KEY #15

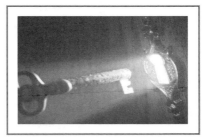

DELIVERANCE THROUGH THE TITHE

"I will rebuke the devourer for your sakes, so that he will not destroy the fruit of your ground, nor shall the vine fail to bear fruit for you in the field,"
says the LORD of hosts.
—Malachi 3:11

S atan gains advantage over everyone who places themselves outside of the will of God by disobeying His Word.

When we hear the Word of God, become convicted, repent from our sins, receive Christ, and return to God, many aspects of our lives experience change. In our conversation, we will stop swearing and lying, and we will begin speaking encouraging, wise, and powerful words. Our sick conversation will be healed. We will stop cheating on our wives or husbands. We will stop stealing. We will become great employees. We will apologize to those we have wronged. We will get our lives right with our neighbors, our God, and ourselves. We will commit ourselves to attend church. We will commit ourselves to prayer and the study of the Bible. Eventually, we get right with God in nearly every single area. Yet, He still says, *"Return to Me."* Why does He say this? Because we need to get right with God *financially*, as well all of those other areas.

> *"Yet from the days of your fathers You have gone away from My ordinances and have not kept them. Return to Me, and I will return to you," says the LORD of hosts. "But you said, 'In what way shall we return?' Will a man rob God? Yet you have robbed Me! But you say, 'In what way have we robbed You?' In tithes and offerings."* (Malachi 3:7–8)

To be right with God financially means to pay our tithes and give offerings to God—not just offerings and not just tithes, but *both*, as the Scripture above indicates. Tithes belong to God. If we are found with them in our hand, we are considered to be robbing from God. We cannot expect a financial breakthrough in our lives if we are stealing from God or withholding from Him what He has requested from us.

In 2 Thessalonians 3:11, Paul calls people who don't work, *"disorderly."* He says these people should get a job so they will have something to give. Some people will say, "I'm no thief," yet they don't tithe. Withholding from God places them among the very worst of thieves—those who take from God Himself! If we are not tithing, then we are stealing from God and from His house. Plain and simple.

The church is not an "organization," it is a congregation of the people of God. If we as a body fail to bring the tithes and offerings, which belong to God, then as a church we are not right with Him. Once we have gotten right with God in this area, the curse brought on by withholding the tithe will be removed.

We must never be found to be withholding from God. Everyone must play a part in bringing the incredible financial breakthrough God intends to bring to His church. The breakthrough in the church begins in our spirits. When we break free from holding back the tithe, we will cause a breakthrough in the heavens

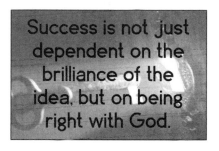

Success is not just dependent on the brilliance of the idea, but on being right with God.

over our lives so that such blessings will begin to fall upon us all that we won't be able to contain them!

> *"And I will rebuke the devourer for your sakes, so that he will not destroy the fruit of your ground, nor shall the vine fail to bear fruit for you in the field," says the LORD of hosts.* (Malachi 3:11)

The Tithe Defeats the Destroyer

The Israelites were a farming community whose financial prosperity depended on their crops becoming ripe for harvest. However, there were many different diseases and pestilences that could prevent that from happening. Blasting hot east winds that dried and ruined crops and mildew fungus on plants were just two of the calamities that could come upon their farmlands and destroy their economy. The Lord declared this to be the work of a personality called *"the devourer."*

When we fail to tithe, the door to the devil is left wide open. The *"devourer"* is able to gain access to the resources and provisions of our lives and *"destroy"* them.

———

The devourer can get into anyone's business and wreak havoc. When we tithe from our business income, our forms of income are protected from destruction. Instead of business deals falling through, the "vine bears fruit." God will rebuke the devil for you once your tithes have been paid to Him. Projects will not keep failing. They will come to fruition. Plans will be successful, and the curse will be removed.

> *"Your crops will be large, for I will guard them from insects and plagues. Your grapes won't shrivel away before they ripen,"* says the Lord Almighty.
>
> (Malachi 3:11 TLB)

This thief is not restricted to the world of agriculture. The devourer is a "he," a person. In John 10:10, Jesus called the destroyer *"the thief"*: *"The thief* [the devil] *does not come except to steal, and to kill, and to destroy."* The purpose of the destroyer is to steal all the blessings of God from every believer's life. Success is not just dependent on the brilliance of the plan or the idea, but on being right with God. This leads to His blessing on all that we do.

———

When Jesus rebukes something, it is *gone!*

✓ In Mark 4:39 He rebuked the wind, and it ceased. He rebuked the stormy seas, and they calmed.

✓ In Mark 9:25 He rebuked the demon of deafness, and it left the boy.

✓ In Matthew 17:18 He rebuked a self-destructive spirit out of a boy, and it left him.

✓ In Mark 1:25 He rebuked an unclean spirit out of a person in the synagogue, and it left him.

✓ In Luke 4:39 He rebuked the fever in Peter's mother-in-law, and it left her.

When God rebukes the devourer from our lives, the devourer *must leave!* Instead of continually losing, we start winning. Our finances get healthy. The destroyer is destroyed!

KEY #16

FIRSTFRUITS

*Honor the LORD with your possessions, and with
the firstfruits of all your increase; so your barns
will be filled with plenty, and your vats will
overflow with new wine.*
—Proverbs 3:9–10

The promises of God remain sure. I am often asked by
people who are already tithing on their salary if they
need to also tithe on their inheritance, or on their
bonus, or on income from shares of stocks, interest, profit on
assets, sales, etc.

Proverbs 3:9 says that we are to honor the Lord with the
firstfruits of *all* our increase. This means that we do not just
tithe only on the cash that turns up in our paycheck. We need
to be honest before God about the extent of our *"increase"*
and bring the firstfruits of all of that increase to Him. *Anything whatsoever* that brings us increase, we need to bring
the firstfruits of that increase to the Lord. The firstfruits

is the first 10 percent of my increase—whatever comes in my door, whatever is given into my hands, whatever I earn. No matter where the income is from, if our finances or possessions are increased, then we need to tithe on that. If we receive benefits that are not cash but have a commensurate cash value such as rent or health benefits paid for by an employer, then we need to calculate the cash value and tithe on that.

———◇———

Recently, my wife and I sold our house during the process of buying a new one. After I had calculated all of the figures, we arranged a new loan and proceeded with the purchase. One night, lying in bed, I suddenly realized that I hadn't factored in the tithe on the profit from the sale of our old house! When I realized that, I discovered I was short by more than $20,000. So I made a commitment to God to pay it off over the next twelve months (it ended up taking six).

Some would argue that we had tithed on all the income that purchased that house in the first place and that we were therefore free from having to tithe on the profit. Wrong! The profit *was* increase—an extra amount that came to us that didn't exist before.

I never try to argue myself out of tithing, because I know that God will only bless us as we place Him first in every detail of our financial lives. My wife and I have always found our "barns full" and our "vats overflowing." The firstfruits of all our increase belong to God.

———◇———

Some people ask me if they should tithe on the net or the gross amount. I tell them I'm the wrong person to ask if they're looking for an easy answer. God should come first, before the government, in His claim on our finances. I'll bet Jesus is pretty weary of being at the end of the line, waiting for our meager leftovers. He shouldn't even be *in* the line! He gets the first of all our income, not the IRS, not the medical insurers, not the bills, not the kids, not the vacation, not the recreational vehicles. Our tithe comes from *all* the money

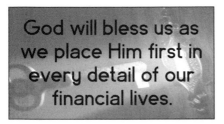
God will bless us as we place Him first in every detail of our financial lives.

we earn, which includes the amount we earn that goes to pay our income taxes. In simple terms, my answer is that we should tithe on our gross income, which means *all* of our income—whether it is gifts, benefits, dividends, earned income—anything that brings financial increase to us. One-tenth of it all belongs to God. That's not too much to ask of a God who gave it all to us in the first place.

We must realize that tithing is only the beginning of giving. Once we have given God the tithe that belongs to Him, we can then begin to give offerings to the Lord that are above and beyond the tithe...and bring above and beyond abundance!

THE LAWS OF
HARVEST LIVING

KEY #17

LAW ONE:
GIVING IS SOWING

He who sows...
—2 Corinthians 9:6

P aul takes pains to reveal the reality of giving. He calls it "sowing and reaping." Giving is *sowing seed*. That is not a metaphor; it is not *like* sowing seed, it is actually sowing something. In the way that we sow seeds into the ground, we can do the same with our money. The simple act of *giving* is what establishes our money as seed sown. Investing our money in land, banks, shares, or bonds is not sowing. Sowing is giving to God, to His church, and to people in need.

The Seed Principle

God has designed the natural and the spiritual world to run on the seed principle. The entire kingdom of God operates on the seed principle: Unless a seed is sown, it has no power to reproduce. When the seed is sown, its amazing, miraculous power goes to work.

Seeds were found in the ancient Egyptian tomb of King Tutankhamen, who was buried along with many treasures over three thousand years ago. Yet, in all that time, those seeds accomplished absolutely nothing. After being found, some of them were planted in the fertile soil on the banks of the Nile. It wasn't long before they sprang up and produced a harvest of fruitful plants. All the time the seeds were in the tomb  they remained barren. Once planted, they began to do the impossible: they blossomed to life and produced thousands more seeds than they started with—all that after lying dormant and useless for three thousand years!

The apostle Paul is not attempting to give us a lesson in agriculture. He is telling us that as soon as we give the seed, we release the miracle. What we give becomes a seed in the soil of heaven and will inevitably return to us as a bountiful harvest!

KEY #18

LAW TWO:
GOD SUPPLIES SEED
TO THE SOWER

*He who supplies seed to the sower, and bread for
food, supply and multiply the seed you have sown.*
—2 Corinthians 9:10

God supplies seed to the sower. Some think that when
they have enough money, then they will begin giving. They are missing the point! The route to having enough is in giving what you have *now*. *As we sow* is
when God supplies more seed for us to sow!

Some people say that when they get a million dollars,
they'll give it to the church. I would say they should give
the hundred they have in their pockets right now, and
they'll have a better chance of attaining that million they're
dreaming about. Inevitably, many people have an excuse

as to why they can't give now, and I inevitably never see those people actually bring in the millions—much less the hundreds. In general, the talkers don't give and the givers don't talk.

On the positive side, I've also seen people make a commitment to sow into a ministry even though they do not yet have the money. They want to give, and they genuinely make a heartfelt commitment and put in a pledge. Then God begins to move, and they find themselves in a new realm of supply.

Each year my wife and I make a new commitment to our church's building fund. We make *giving* goals, not just getting goals. As we do this, God supplies seed. He has promised to supply seed to the sower, to those committed to giving to the house of God.

The Way of the Sower

Being a sower is moving from the verb to the noun. It is moving from doing something to *being* something. Being a sower means that giving is a lifestyle, it's the *purpose* of living. It isn't just about sowing seed, it's about *becoming a sower*. It is a way of life. You become known as a sower. As a sower, you also become a perpetual harvester because sowers are always reaping as they sow.

> *Now may He who supplies seed to the sower, and bread for food, supply and multiply the seed you have sown and increase the fruits of your righteousness.*
> (2 Corinthians 9:10)

Once we commit ourselves to being sowers, God ensures that we have seed for sowing. This commitment to give to the church and to ministries will bring to us the seed for sowing.

During the times in our church when we have raised money for building projects, some people get very excited about what they will give. Sometimes they get too excited and want to give beyond their real faith. When they approach me, the conversation goes something like this:

Once we commit to being sowers, God ensures that we have seed for sowing.

"Pastor, we decided we want to give $50,000 to the project."

"That's wonderful. How will you do that?" I ask.

"By faith, Pastor—by faith," they assure me. "We believe God will supply it."

"I see," I respond. "How much do you guys earn?"

"Well, between the two of us, around seventy-five thousand bucks. My wife earns around twenty-five thousand, and I earn fifty."

"Well, you could give her wage over a two year period, and you'd be able to do it."

"Uh...nope, can't do that. We're totally committed with rent, bills, schooling, medical insurance—heck, we don't have a penny to spare."

"Okay, but that's where *God* will supply. You did say you have faith for the fifty thousand to come in. Right?"

"But not like that! I mean, give up her salary for two whole years?!"

That's when the reality check on their faith suddenly clicks in.

When people are faced with the reality of the true level of their faith, they often find their excitement level has exceeded their determination to carry through with their commitment. So, I say to those people, "Let's rethink the amount then. What about five thousand dollars? Can you handle that?"

"Well, sure. Yes, yes, we could drop the vacation and not get the new refrigerator..."

Now they are in faith—they *know* they can do it. Once they make that commitment, inevitably, the following week will come and they will inform me that the very week after they took that step in faith, he got a $2,500 raise and their child received a scholarship that will pay her school fees for the next two years. They suddenly find that their entire commitment has been covered.

God will always faithfully supply seed to sowers who identify exactly how they will sow. That is how He grows our faith. That way, a couple like this will be able to believe at a higher level next time around, and God's supply will likewise increase.

KEY #19

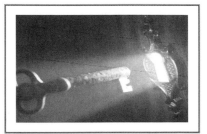

LAW THREE:
WHAT YOU SOW IS
WHAT YOU REAP

Give, and it will be given to you.
—Luke 6:38

In the above Scripture, the *"it"* given to us is what we give. What we give is what will return to us. This is obvious. Take the example of a seed: When we plant an apple seed, we don't expect to harvest peaches. If we plant corn seeds, then corn is what we will harvest. It becomes important, then, to understand what we want to harvest. The kind of harvest you want determines the seed you need to sow.

If you want more time, then you sow time to God, in serving Him. If you want more friendships, then you sow your friendship to others. If pastors want more people in church, then they should give people to the work of the Lord in other places. If we want a harvest of money, then we need to sow money. Whatever we sow we will reap.

As believers, we seek to meet the needs we are presented with. If we have what people need, then that is what we are called to give. We are channels of provision from God to the people of this world. If God can get it *through* us, He will get it *to* us.

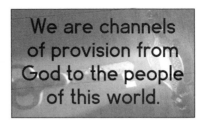

We are channels of provision from God to the people of this world.

KEY #20

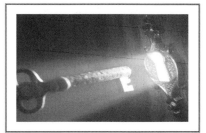

LAW FOUR:
WHERE YOU SOW IS
WHERE YOU REAP

*Blessed are you who sow beside all waters, who send
out freely the feet of the ox and the donkey.*
—Isaiah 32:20

The blessing of God will cover our entire lives if we
sow throughout all the areas of our lives. If we sow at
church, at home, at work, at play, with friends, with
strangers, we will also reap in all of those areas. Wherever
the waters of God are flowing for us, we should sow.

Every day we should scheme to bless someone. If we
spend our days giving, we will also spend our days reaping.
If giving is an infrequent event for us, then reaping will also
be infrequent. If we give in only one or two areas, then we
will reap in only one or two areas. The farmer who sows seed

by all the streams on his land and not just the main river, will reap by all the streams, not just the main river.

Isaiah 32:20 also speaks of giving without prejudice. There are many streams that we are not involved in personally, but it doesn't mean we should not be sowing into those streams. If we sow into streams other than our own, we will reap from streams other than our own.

Isaiah says the person who sows beside all waters will be blessed. That applies to those who send out ministries all over the world. When we sow every day, in every given situation, we will be continuously reaping in every situation.

Every Good Work

God is able to make all grace abound toward you, that you, always having all sufficiency in all things, may have an abundance for every good work.
(2 Corinthians 9:8)

In the above Scripture, Paul says that God is able to make *all* grace *abound* toward us so that we will have *all* sufficiency in *all* things, and we will have an *abundance for every good work*. That may be the most sweeping promise in the entire Bible. All the grace of God abounds toward the generous believer so they will have all they need in every area of their lives. They will have enough cars, houses, clothes, money, food, and everything else necessary to enable them to get involved in every good work. That applies not just on payday, or once a year, or once a month, but every day—morning, noon, and night. We should be perpetually able to contribute to, and get involved in, every good work that comes our way.

When the general offering for the tithe comes, we give. When the building fund comes, we give. When the missions fund offering comes, we give. When the love offering comes, we give. When the special offering comes, we give. When we meet people in need, we give. When we simply want to be generous and bless people, we give.

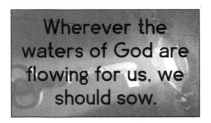

Wherever the waters of God are flowing for us, we should sow.

Sowers are never in a position where they are unable to give, because of the abundance that God has supplied them with for every good work—which is everywhere they sow.

KEY #21

LAW FIVE:
THE QUALITY YOU SOW IS
THE QUALITY YOU REAP

"And when you offer the blind as a sacrifice, Is it not evil? And when you offer the lame and sick, Is it not evil? Offer it then to your governor! Would he be pleased with you? Would he accept you favorably?" says the LORD of hosts. "You also say, 'Oh, what a weariness!' And you sneer at it," says the LORD of hosts. "And you bring the stolen, the lame, and the sick; thus you bring an offering! Should I accept this from your hand?" says the LORD.
—Malachi 1:8, 13

I n the verse above, Malachi had been scrutinizing the offerings that the people were bringing to God. This happened several times in Scripture. Even Jesus investigated what people were giving at the temple, and He brought teaching from what He observed.

In Acts 5, Peter asked the people about the offerings they were bringing. One couple was attempting to look as though they were giving 100 percent, but actually they were not. They had conspired to bring a smaller percentage of their money, but to tell the apostles they were bringing everything. When Peter asked them if they had given everything, they tried to deceive the man of God. The Holy Spirit gave Peter insight into the deception, telling him that the couple had lied to God, and both fell down dead before the Lord.

Malachi observed that some of the people were bringing sick, blind, lame, or stolen animals for their offering. Some had vowed they would bring a certain animal, but when it came time to fulfill the vow, they decided not to bring the healthy beast, but rather some sick old cow.

They throw a blanket over ol' Betsy, who has one eye missing and can't see out of the other. The tractor had run over her back leg. She's bony and suffering from tooth rot. Can't sell her, can't get milk out of her, can't eat her, may as well sacrifice her. They bring the old cow down to the temple, slip the priest a few hundred denari, and offer up this sick animal as an offering to God, thinking they can pull a fast one. However, the prophet sees what's going on, and he rebukes the people and the priests for their less-than-spotless offering.

It is a travesty to give God a shabby offering. Sometimes, people think that God should be happy if they give Him anything at all. But that is not the case. Our offering is just that—an offering. There is no guarantee that God will accept our offering. If He accepts it, then we will receive blessing upon our lives; if not, we won't. There is a way to ensure that our offerings are acceptable and actually *pleasing* to Him: by giving exactly what He calls us to give.

In the book of Malachi, the worshippers were bringing offerings to God that were unacceptable. They were offering things they would rather get rid of, or things they no longer needed. There was no cost to the giver.

These days, people bring things to the church that no longer work to see if the church has any use for them. They bring an old car they are going to dump, thinking there may be someone at church who can use it, or an old typewriter or an outdated computer with parts that don't function any more. We need to have a higher view of God. Give those old beat-up, trash-bound things to the devil! Let him have the 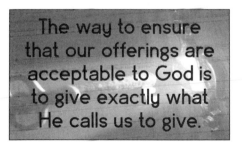 junk! The church is not the local garbage heap. It is a place where we give the best offerings to God, things of unblemished quality that reflect His glory.

Our offerings should not be found sick, lying in the bottom of the offering plate in need of a respirator and a blood transfusion. They need to be healthy, vigorous offerings that can accomplish something for His kingdom. Our offerings must have vision, knowing that what we are giving is going to do something great for God. We need to be able to give an offering that stands tall and walks, not something that limps and shuffles along. Sadly, that is more often how the church has functioned—limping along because of weak offerings.

When my wife and I came to Christ, we got rid of everything we felt uncomfortable about in our new life, and that left us with very little. We had no radio, no television, hardly any books, and just one really nice guitar that we would play and sing worship songs with.

One day a friend came by and was admiring our guitar. I told him he could have it. I wanted to give it to him because he liked it so much. Since that time, about thirty years ago, we have had guitars of all kinds given to us. All of them have been very high quality guitars. Sometimes we even get guitars in the mail! The amazing thing is that we now have children who write, sing, and record music. They also have guitars given to them. From one seed, we have unleashed a "guitar tree" that keeps on yielding, even through to our children.

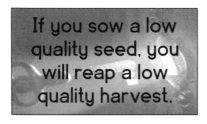

If you sow a low quality seed, you will reap a low quality harvest.

When we left New Zealand to come to Australia, I gave away a bruised and battered old surfboard. When we arrived in Australia, I was given a surfboard that was yellowed, dinged, and beaten up. I decided then and there that the only things worth giving are of high quality.

When we sow low quality seed, we reap a low quality harvest. If you want to reap the best, give the best!

KEY #22

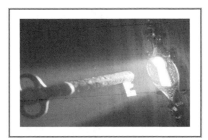

LAW SIX:
THE MEASURE YOU SOW IS
THE MEASURE YOU REAP

*Give, and it will be given to you: good measure,
pressed down, shaken together, and running over will
be put into your bosom. For with the same measure
that you use, it will be measured back to you.*
—Luke 6:38

The measure of your giving will be the measure of your reaping. If you give an abundance of what you have, then you will receive an abundance of what God has. If you give a little of what you have, then you will receive only a little of what God has. The level of abundance to be measured out to you is in *your* hands.

Giving has less to do with total amounts than with ratios. Jesus revealed this when He commended the poor widow who gave just a tiny total compared to others, observing that she actually gave *more* than all the others because she gave *all* she had. The rich announced their gifts with great pomp and ceremony, but Jesus chided them because even though the amounts were large and impressive, they only represented a tiny percentage of their total worth.

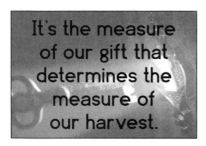

It's the measure of our gift that determines the measure of our harvest.

The building fund slogan of our church is, "Not equal giving, but equal sacrifice." We understand that for some people, one thousand dollars is a lot of money, while for others one hundred thousand is a relatively small amount.

I have heard leaders present their vision and the amount they hope to raise, and then tell everyone that if they divide it up by the number of people in their congregation everyone will have to give only so much. For some, however, that amount is far too large, and for others it's nothing. And even then, not everyone is going to give to that particular project.

Generally, in a building project, around 10 percent of the targeted amount comes from one or two individuals, another 30 percent from a small group of leading givers, another 20 to 30 percent from the leaders of the congregation, and the balance from the rest of the people.

The Measure

It's the measure of our gift, not the amount, that determines the measure of our harvest. If a farmer wants to harvest a thousand plants but sows only one hundred seeds, he is going to be disappointed. No matter if he prays, fasts, and confesses God's promises till his tongue falls out, if he has sown one hundred seeds that is how many plants he is going to reap.

The concept is beautiful in its simplicity: When you sow abundantly, you reap abundantly. When you sow sparsely, you reap sparsely.

Key #23

Law Seven:
The Seed Multiplies

*Now may He who supplies seed to the sower,
and bread for food, supply and multiply the
seed you have sown and increase
the fruits of your righteousness.*
—2 Corinthians 9:10

No farmer on earth plants a seed and expects to get only one seed back for the effort. He anticipates a plant that will yield at least a hundred times the seed he put in. When we plant seed in God, we can also anticipate that He will multiply it—often greatly.

When we first started our church in Sydney, my wife Chris needed to travel to New Zealand to visit her mother, who was a widow and disliked flying. But we didn't have the money for Chris to travel. So Chris went to the travel agent, booked the tickets, and got ready to go. The agent kept ringing up, asking when we were going to pay. But we had agreed to trust God, so we didn't cancel the trip.

In the middle of this process, Chris came across an article in a Christian magazine questioning the whole issue of Christians expecting to receive finances from the Lord. This knocked her faith around a bit. We talked about it. We studied the Scriptures again and soon became fully confident that God actually enjoys supplying the needs of His children.

Over that weekend, just a few days before Chris was due to fly, a gentleman in our church approached Chris and told her he felt the urge to loan (not give) her the amount she needed for the tickets. Meanwhile, my brother, who had been living with us, had also returned

When we plant seed in God, we can also expect that He will multiply it.

to New Zealand and left his car with us so we could sell it for him. He said it was only worth around eight hundred dollars, but that we could have the proceeds to pay for the ticket. We knew we could cover the loan by selling the car.

Another person in our church heard that we were trying to sell the car, and he offered to buy it to give to a couple in the church who needed a car. However, he didn't yet have the money to buy one for the couple. So, we said he could have the car and pay us later. In the meantime, we invited the couple needing a car around to our house for a meal. After the meal, we gave them the keys to the car and told them someone in the church had bought it for them.

A couple of weeks later, after Chris had returned from New Zealand, the man who had agreed to buy the vehicle for the couple brought the money to the church and gave it to Chris. Chris then sought out the other man who had originally loaned her the eight hundred dollars and gave him the money. As it happened, on that particular Sunday we were holding a building fund offering for the new premises we were moving into. When Chris handed him the money, he told her to put it into the building fund instead!

That is an amazing story because it shows God multiplying seed when we step out in faith. Chris got to visit her mother in New Zealand with the kids, a young couple got a much needed car, the building fund got eight hundred dollars, and three people got to sow seed that would produce a harvest in their own lives. All from faith, obedience, and a used car.

But others fell on good ground and yielded a crop: some a hundredfold, some sixty, some thirty.
(Matthew 13:8)

If a farmer reaps ten acres this year but next year wants to reap one hundred acres, he obviously needs to sow more this year than he sowed last year. If he sows another ten-acre field from his harvest, no matter how much he prays, believes, or confesses, his capacity to reap remains limited to what he has sown. If, however, he takes enough seed from his last harvest to sow a one hundred acre area, he will achieve his goal of reaping one hundred acres.

When we start giving according to the measure we expect to receive, we break through into a greater measure of harvesting.

Our seed multiplies at varying levels, but the lowest level the Word promises is thirty-fold (Matthew 13:8). No

THE LAWS OF HARVEST LIVING

bank or investment firm on earth would promise those kind of rates as its lowest return! And to promise a maximum of a hundredfold would be utterly crazy! Even we as believers have trouble accepting those figures. We seem to be able to accept that maybe the Lord would multiply our seed times ten, but to think that we can sow ten and reap a thousand seems too incredible to be true! But we *must believe it* if

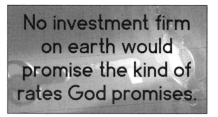

No investment firm on earth would promise the kind of rates God promises.

we are to see the kind of harvest God wants for us in this hour. The message: *Sow to your harvest!*

KEY #24

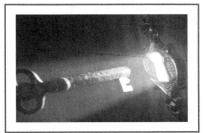

LAW EIGHT:
THE SEED MUST BE
PLANTED IN THE GROUND

*Most assuredly, I say to you, unless a grain of wheat
falls into the ground and dies, it remains alone; but if it
dies, it produces much grain.*
—John 12:24

Our sowing seed must be given away completely—it
must be planted *in the ground.*

At one of my birthdays as a youngster, a friend
gave me a birthday present but said he would have to come
and get it back after a week. When I opened it up, it was a
chemistry set with all kinds of amazing things inside. My
little friend had obviously seen the gift and wanted to keep
it far more than he wanted to give it, so he planned on taking it back. I can't remember him ever coming to reclaim his

"gift," but I have seen a lot of people give something...but not *really* give it. There are all kinds of invisible strings attached to some gifts. But that should never be the case. A gift is a gift is a gift!

When a farmer plants a seed in the soil, he doesn't tie a piece of string around it or dig it up to see what's happening to it. Giving must be *pure* (*"with simplicity,"* as it says in the King James Version of Romans 12:8), otherwise it ceases to be sowing, and the harvest is therefore hampered. To give is to "relinquish control," to "let go of completely," and to allow the recipient to assume complete control and responsibility for what he has received.

I sometimes hear teaching that talks about sowing into "good soil." I must admit, although the agricultural concept is true, I don't buy into the idea that a ministry is either good or bad soil. The soil in which you plant a seed is not who or what you give to on earth, but to God in heaven. There have been thousands of people who have given millions of dollars to ministries that have collapsed for one reason or another, through immorality or bad management or other factors. If all of those people were to believe that their seed only had a chance if it were planted in "good soil" (in other words, healthy ministry), then their faith for a harvest would be severely damaged. Don't worry about judging the quality of the soil! Worry more about the quality of the *seed*. God may be tilling up the soil in His own timing. In the meantime, He will bless the intention of your heart with your seed.

Some ministries claim to be "good soil" into which people can plant their seed, but it is difficult to establish a scriptural basis for this concept. Nevertheless, when we give from a good motive and with a cheerful attitude, no matter to whom or what on earth we are giving, we are actually giving to the Lord. In fact, no matter what happens to the money we give, if we have given it to God, it is in good ground. He has received our offering.

> *Here mortal men receive tithes, but there he receives them, of whom it is witnessed that He lives.*
>
> (Hebrews 7:8)

After winning a tournament, the great Argentine golfer Robert De Vincenzo received the prize check and, smiling for the cameras, he went to the clubhouse and prepared to leave. A little while later, he walked alone to his car in the parking lot and was approached by a young woman. She congratulated him on his victory and then told him that her child was seriously ill and near death. She did not know how she could pay the doctor's bills and hospital expenses. De Vincenzo was touched by her story, and he took out a pen and endorsed his winning check over to the woman. "Make some good days for the baby," he encouraged her as he pressed the check into her hand.

Don't worry about the quality of the soil. Concentrate on the quality of the seed.

The next week he was having lunch in a country club when a Professional Golf Association official came to his table. "Some of the boys in the parking lot last week told me you met a young woman there after you won that tournament," he said.

De Vincenzo nodded.

"Well," said the official, "I have news for you: she's a phony. She has no sick baby. She's not even married. She fleeced you, my friend."

"You mean...there's no dying baby?" De Vincenzo exclaimed.

"That's right," said the official, "no dying baby."

De Vincenzo thought for a second and then smiled. "That's the best news I've heard all week!" he said.

———————

It is God Himself who is the "soil" our seed is planted into. Our attitude is the "climate" that surrounds the planting of that seed. And no matter what people do with the money we give, we can rest assured God will give us a great harvest! Those who handle money given to the work of the Lord will have to give an account of it to the Lord. When we give, we relinquish control of how that money is used, knowing before God that we have fulfilled our part. The rest is in His hands...and what better place could our seed be in!

He who has pity on the poor lends to the LORD, and
He will pay back what he has given.

(Proverbs 19:17)

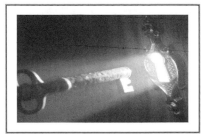

KEY #25

LAW NINE: THE SEED MUST BE LEFT ALONE FOR THE HARVEST TO OCCUR

Take heed that you do not do your charitable deeds before men, to be seen by them. Otherwise you have no reward from your Father in heaven. Therefore, when you do a charitable deed, do not sound a trumpet before you as the hypocrites do in the synagogues and in the streets, that they may have glory from men. Assuredly, I say to you, they have their reward.
—Matthew 6:1–2

J esus looks at the *motive* behind our giving. The only motive He condemns is when we seek to impress others with our giving. He doesn't condemn us when we give in order to reap a harvest. Some people feel they are very pious when they announce that they don't give in order to get, but only for the honor of giving. However, the Lord does not have a problem with giving in order to reap a harvest. In fact, in Luke 6, He teaches this very principle to *motivate* us to give:

> *Give, and it will be given to you: good measure, pressed down, shaken together, and running over will be put into your bosom. For with the same measure that you use, it will be measured back to you.* (Luke 6:38)

When we give with the intention that others will notice, we are not really sowing, we are just dropping seed out in the open for others to see. Seed sown in soil cannot be seen. And for it to grow, it must remain hidden. If a person who has sown seed keeps pulling it out for everyone to see, that seed will never grow. We will not reap a harvest from seed sown to gain people's admiration or attention.

When you sow the seed, leave it alone! The power of God will go to work on it, just like the soil goes to work on a seed that is planted in the ground.

———◇———

At our church, whenever we host a building fund or if I am seeking to raise people's faith in the areas of giving and receiving, I ask people who have been blessed to testify about it. Sometimes they are hesitant to tell others what they have given. I urge them to tell how, when, and how much they gave, so that others will be inspired. Without these testimonies, my experience has shown that the program will be only half as successful. As people hear what happened in the lives of others, they increase their own giving or are inspired to keep on going when they feel like giving up.

There is tremendous power in testimony. In Matthew 5:16, Jesus told us there are times when we should let our good works be seen by men so they will glorify God. There is nothing wrong in announcing what we have given. It's all about our *motivation*. If we want to impress others with our giving, then that's all we'll do and that's all we'll get in return. However, when our motivation is to *inspire* others to give because of our own testimony, then our seed remains sown in the ground, ready to grow and produce a great harvest.

The Harvest Always Takes Time

And let us not grow weary while doing good, for in due season we shall reap if we do not lose heart.
(Galatians 6:9)

There is an entire season of life between sowing and reaping. The apostle Paul says that we will reap if we do not faint. People tend to *"faint"* in prayer, in doing good works, and in faith. They give up and fade out.

No farmer waits until he has a need for food before he starts sowing seed. There is no such thing as an instant harvest in the agricultural world. For the most part, that analogy holds true in the principle of giving, too. It's not enough to start giving when we suddenly have a need, hoping for an instant harvest. We must be sowing *all the time*. That way, when we do have a need, the seed has already been sown, and we can reap our harvest.

Most harvests take a lot longer than we anticipate for them to ripen, but they prove well worth the wait!

In Galatians 6:9, Paul talks of continuing to *"do good."* The context is about supporting the ministry of those who teach us the Word of God. Continuing to do good is continuing to give. It is "not fainting" and not giving up on giving. When we tire of giving, we cease to provide the proper climate for cultivating and nourishing the seed we have sown, and it is hindered from growing to a full harvest. The best climate to encourage growth from seed we've sown is the climate of *giving.*

We live in a fast-food, instant society. Once upon a time we had to collect wood for the fire, stoke up the stove, prepare the food, and then cook it for hours in a crude oven—which could take up to half a day. Now, however, we grab a precooked dinner, nuke it in the microwave, and stand over the thing while it spins around, tapping the countertop and wondering why these things take so long.

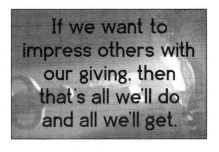

If we want to impress others with our giving, then that's all we'll do and all we'll get.

God does not move at the same pace as our present world. Part of our problem is this "fast pace, low grace" society we've developed from attempting to cram so much into so little time. In this great rush to live life quickly, it's easy to become impatient with the pace at which God moves. We need to learn the art of patience: maintaining a good attitude while we wait longer than we want to for God to do what He wants to.

As we cultivate our soil and maintain a giving climate over our seed, our *"due season"* will come!

Rest in the Lord, and wait patiently for Him.
(Psalm 37:7)

PRINCIPLES OF PRODUCTIVITY

KEY #26

GOD BLESSES THE WORK OF OUR HANDS

And may the Lord our God show us his approval
and make our efforts successful. Yes, make
our efforts successful!
—Psalm 90:17 NLT

So far we have focused on giving as the key foundation for a financially excellent life. Giving alone, however, does not encapsulate the entire principle. There is more to having a financially sound life than simply giving.

Some Christians have concluded that giving is all there is to prospering in life. The idea that if people simply give, they will automatically receive abundance in their lives is faulty. Certain other elements are essential in order for us prosper. Generating great income requires more than merely giving.

Scripture encourages those in the kingdom of God to be people of wealth. We are instructed on how to assist the poor, not on how to become poor. The obvious inference of the Scripture is that we should be in a position to help the poor. We should have more than enough for ourselves, so that as people of God's kingdom we are able to express His love for the poor with very real and practical help.

Proverbs 13:22 says that the wealth of the wicked will be stored up for the righteous. However, this wealth doesn't just fall into our laps. It must be earned, created, cultivated. *Wealth creation* must become the way we live.

I've known people who are faithful in tithing and generous in giving, yet they still do not experience abundance in their lives. What generally confuses people is not what is said with regard to finances, it is what is *not* said. Although we may desire it to be so, having God in our lives doesn't relieve us from life's normal processes. God is not a way out of our responsibilities. 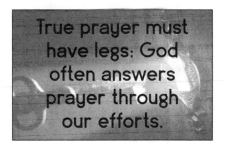 He's not some enormous lucky charm in our lives, protecting us from harm and bringing us good. Too many Christians are under the impression that if we ask God to do something, He will simply do it, as if that's all there is to prayer. But true prayer must have *legs*: God more often answers our prayers through our *efforts*. As we move, He moves. He blesses the work of our hands. He empowers and helps us in many different ways as we continue His work until our prayers are answered.

We must not merely be motivated by the end results we are hoping for, but instead we must live with respect and love for God. We must include God in the approach we take to life, or our lives simply will not work. Likewise, there will be times when we will need to be willing to jeopardize the end result because we have chosen to take a stand for integrity. Relationships may be placed under threat because we refuse to be party to investments or involvements that are unjust.

Excellence becomes ours when pleasing God means more to us than money itself. The end result of this is that we will not only prosper, but we will also enjoy the journey, with the peace of God reigning in our hearts.

When money is more important than God, people sacrifice their integrity to the "dollar god." They lay down their health on the altar of money, sacrificing their health to that cruel god. Their marriages are thrown to the fire in serving that exacting god. And what does that god deliver? Time and again, we hear about those who have made it to "the top" only to find it bleak and empty, because they lost their souls in the process.

There is nothing in this life with so much value that it is worth the sacrifice of your soul. Once that reality is firmly planted in your life, you will prosper *from the inside out!*

Work Enables Us to Fulfill Our Dreams

Dreams without work are doomed. Knowing that "God provides" does not excuse us from hard work. Tithing is not a substitute for effort.

Work is its own reward, because giving to God ensures that whatever we put our hand to will enjoy success—if not at first, then eventually. When God planted Adam and Eve in the garden of Eden, He didn't draw up an employment contract with them. He didn't offer them a salary package for tending the trees. The work itself was intended to be their *lifestyle*—which was itself their reward.

Work is something God intended for us to enjoy. It is a *calling* from God. Avoiding work is avoiding God's provision for our health and well-being. A negative attitude toward work will leave you poor. Some people see work as a necessary evil. Given the choice, too many people would rather not work. Yet there's more therapy, wholeness, and self-respect gained through honest work than through any other means. If we settle the fact that basically we will work throughout our lives, then that mind-set will lead us on a path of prosperity.

Diligence

The soul of the diligent shall be made rich.

(Proverbs 13:4)

God looks for diligent, hardworking people He can send with His message to a hungry world. If we don't go to work to get God's message out to the lost, then we are simply distasteful and annoying to Him.

The hand of the diligent will rule. (Proverbs 12:24)

The *American Heritage Dictionary* defines diligence as: *1. Earnest and persistent application to an undertaking; steady effort; assiduity. 2. Attentive care; heedfulness.*

Leadership falls to those who are diligent. People who are not diligent find themselves having to work for someone else. Diligence is assuming your responsibility, meeting your deadlines, keeping your promises, preparing thoroughly all the areas of your business, fulfilling requirements, and persisting until the project is completed.

> *...your work produced by faith, your labor prompted by love, and your endurance inspired by hope in our Lord Jesus Christ.* (1 Thessalonians 1:3 NIV)

According to the Scripture above, your working displays your faith. When you do work, that labor is prompted by love. And when you endure without quitting, it is because you have hope in Jesus. If these tenets hold true, then so do their opposites: if you do not work, then you have no true faith in the Lord! If you are working without faith, then your labor is not prompted by love, but by selfishness or coercion. And when you continue to work in that mind-set of grudging obligation, it is only because you have no hope in Jesus.

We must make sure our work and our desire to work is motivated by faith, love, and hope!

KEY #27

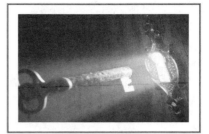

IF WE ARE NOT
PRODUCERS, THEN WE ARE
ONLY CONSUMERS

*Let him who stole steal no longer, but rather let him
labor, working with his hands what is good, that he
may have something to give him who has need.*
—Ephesians 4:28

If we don't produce, then all we do is consume. We need to
ask ourselves whether or not we are putting something
into this life or just taking from it. The great purpose of
prosperity is that we become *useful* to God here on earth.
Are you leaning on people, or are you a dependable resource
whom others can lean on in their time of need?

As believers, we should have an abundance in our lives
so we are able to give to those in need. If we were once those
type of people who tried to get as much as we could for as

little as possible (or even try to get things for free—in other words, to steal), then the Scripture says to do it no longer, but rather to *go to work!*

———————◆———————

Too many Christians these days try to mooch freebees off of their fellow Christians. That attitude cements a *poverty mind-set* into people. We should seek to bless each other in the body. We should be prepared to gift our skills and talents to others in need. However, we should not *expect* or *take* what has not been offered to us, anticipating that just because a person is a Christian they should be helping us for free! That is a taker, a user, a consumer—and not a creator, giver, or producer.

KEY #28

OVERCOMING LAZINESS WILL PROSPER YOUR LIFE

The soul of a lazy man desires, and has nothing.
—Proverbs 13:4

W e are called by Jesus to *build His kingdom*. To "build" means to work. Lazy people do not build. People who refuse to work will destruct rather than construct. There is no neutral ground in the kingdom of God. If we are not building, we are destroying. Too many Christians imagine that they will achieve a lot with a minimum of work. What they fail to recognize is that God won't do for us what we are capable of doing for ourselves.

Each one of us is lazy in some area of our lives. In those areas we will be poor, even though we desire to be successful. We need to identify those areas of laziness and overcome them so we can maximize our potential and harness every possibility God presents to us.

As hard as it may be, the first step in overcoming laziness is to simply admit that we're lazy. The second step is to be around people who work hard. Most of us work better when we work with others. We feel accountable. We get motivated seeing people in action. We see them achieving results, and that spurs us on and helps us to overcome lazy tendencies.

A lazy man buries his hand in the bowl, and will not so much as bring it to his mouth again.

(Proverbs 19:24)

And then there are those who get what they need, but don't actually *apply* it. Like a person who buys the kit furniture to assemble at home, but years later it is still in the spare room. Or like the person who purchases the ingredients for a healthy food lifestyle, but they are gathering dust in the pantry. I wonder how many "excer-cycles" and home gyms are stashed away unopened and unused, simply because the excitement of buying them exceeded the commitment to put them to use.

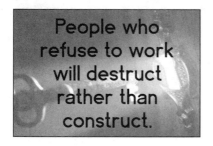

People who refuse to work will destruct rather than construct.

For even when we were with you, we commanded you this: If anyone will not work, neither shall he eat. For we hear that there are some who walk among you in a disorderly manner, not working at all, but are busybodies. Now those who are such we command and exhort through our Lord Jesus Christ that they work in quietness and eat their own bread.

(2 Thessalonians 3:10–12)

Christianity has always held work as sacred. Working hard is part of being a New Testament believer.

In the early church, the apostle Paul referred to Christians who would not work as *"disorderly."* These people had become gossips, meandering through the Christian community talking about other people, not minding their own business, eating other people's food. Paul commanded that if people would not work, neither should they eat. They were not to be catered to by the other Christians; they were to get to work!

He who is slothful in his work is a brother to him who is a great destroyer. (Proverbs 18:9)

Signs of Laziness

There are many signs available to know if you are a lazy person. For example:

1. Lazy people do not acknowledge they are lazy.

The lazy man is wiser in his own eyes than seven men who can answer sensibly. (Proverbs 26:16)

His reasons for not working, for failure, for avoiding work, are all reasonable to himself, and far superior to the combined counsel of seven others.

We are wise to recognize and deal with laziness when we see it in our lives, because laziness brings only poverty.

2. Lazy people love their beds more than they love getting up.

As a door turns on its hinges, so does the lazy man on his bed. (Proverbs 26:14)

3. Lazy people find excuses for not doing things.

The lazy man says, "There is a lion outside! I shall be slain in the streets!" (Proverbs 22:13)

Even when there is no real reason for a lazy person to not work, he will invent one.

In his desperate effort to avoid work, the lazy person makes irrational excuses and reveals his extraordinary selfishness in seeking his own safety and ignoring the peril to others. The righteous person would slay the lion and make the street safe.

4. Laziness causes people to wait for perfect conditions before they get busy.

The lazy man will not plow because of winter; he will beg during harvest and have nothing.
(Proverbs 20:4)

If conditions are harsh, lazy people use them as a reason for inaction. When harvest time comes, since they have sown nothing, they reap nothing. They are left begging.

Laziness has great difficulty in anticipating the future. Even when the future is clear, lazy people don't get ready for it, because they feel no desire to prepare. They are motivated by pressure and desperation. Unless they absolutely have to, lazy people will not act. But by that point, their job will prove to be inadequate, resources wasted, much more effort will have to be invested for a good result, and everybody involved will become frustrated.

5. **Lazy people are not self-starters; they need others to motivate them.**

> *Go to the ant, you sluggard! Consider her ways and be wise, which, having no captain, overseer or ruler, provides her supplies in the summer, and gathers her food in the harvest.*
>
> (Proverbs 6:6–8)

6. **Lazy people don't finish what they start.**

> *The lazy man buries his hand in the bowl; it wearies him to bring it back to his mouth.*
>
> (Proverbs 26:15)

Lazy people buy gym equipment, but never use it. They get the computer program, but fail to load it. They love laying hold of something, but follow-through is unbearably difficult for them to tackle.

> *The lazy man does not roast what he took in hunting, but diligence is man's precious possession.*
> (Proverbs 12:27)

Lazy people never complete a task properly. That is why lazy people reside in an unfinished environment where few things are the way they should be. There is always a mess in their wake. They enjoy the excitement of starting something and the thrill of the pursuit, but if anything more is required, their interest fades at the prospect of the hard work that follows.

The lazy person is simply not interested in the hard part, whereas the diligent embrace it. Getting the job, closing the sale, signing the contract, winning the competition is only the beginning. Sure, we can celebrate, but that is just the start of executing the job.

This applies to leading people to the Lord, as well. A lazy church fails to follow up, doesn't help get new believers established, won't assist in guiding new Christians into ministry, and rarely, if ever, holds them accountable to their calling.

7. **Lazy people annoy those who ask them to do something and are always explaining why it didn't get done.**

Instead of sweet wine, the lazy person is sour vinegar. Instead of a clean fire, they are annoying smoke.

As vinegar to the teeth and smoke to the eyes, so is the lazy man to those who send him.

(Proverbs 10:26)

8. **The lazy person has a chaotic life because nothing is organized, prepared, or planned properly.**

There are too many things left undone for life to flow easily.

The way of the lazy man is like a hedge of thorns, but the way of the upright is a highway.

(Proverbs 15:19)

Getting along with lazy people is always difficult. Lazy people are full of excuses as to why they can't do something or why they didn't do what they were asked. They tend to be prickly and sensitive. They are thorny people who squirm out of their responsibilities. With pointed criticisms and sharp words, they wound the innocent. And as they do, others are wounded too, because the lazy tend to lay blame on others for their own deficiencies and lack of diligence. In this way, they cruelly shift the uncomfortable focus from themselves and onto those around them.

9. **Poverty is the result of laziness.**

> *I went by the field of the lazy man, and by the vineyard of the man devoid of understanding; and there it was, all overgrown with thorns; its surface was covered with nettles; its stone wall was broken down. When I saw it, I considered it well; I looked on it and received instruction: A little sleep, a little slumber, a little folding of the hands to rest; so shall your poverty come like a prowler, and your need like an armed man.*
>
> (Proverbs 24:30–34)

10. **Laziness lets outside influences overwhelm inside desires, which leads to decay and destruction.**

> *Because of laziness the building decays, and through idleness of hands the house leaks.*
>
> (Ecclesiastes 10:18)

11. **Jesus defines laziness as the failure to attempt to realize the potential of the gifts He has given us:**

But his lord answered and said to him, "You wicked and lazy servant, you knew that I reap where I have not sown, and gather where I have not scattered seed." (Matthew 25:26)

12. **While hard workers become the leaders, the lazy man does what he does only because he must or because others put him to it.**

The lazy person has no personal initiative and lacks the motivation to labor unless coerced.

The hand of the diligent will rule, but the lazy man will be put to forced labor. (Proverbs 12:24)

It is only through hard, diligent work that laziness is overcome and our dreams are fulfilled.

Do It Now!

He who observes the wind will not sow, and he who regards the clouds will not reap. (Ecclesiastes 11:4)

The *New Living Translation* interprets the above verse as, *"If you wait for perfect conditions, you will never get anything done."*

If you are waiting for everything to be just right before you give, before you pay your bills, before you buy a house, before you start a business or apply for a job, you'll never see that day. Nothing is ever perfect for what needs to be accomplished. In fact, oftentimes when you decide to take advantage of an opportunity, you will experience great opposition. We can practically gauge the value of the opportunity by the level of opposition against us!

One of the maxims I have bolted to my mind is, *"Do it now!"* It's smart to have an archive of these pithy statements stored in our memories, reminding us to act in certain ways during the various situations throughout our lives. If someone asks me to pray for her, I do it with her right then and there. If someone asks me to phone a person on his behalf, I do it right away. When I receive an assignment, I try to do it immediately, rather than when it is due. I try to pay bills when they arrive, not when they're due. The letter that needs to be written, the invitation that needs to go out, the items on the "to do" list— all should be attacked as soon as possible! That is what helps keep you ahead of the game.

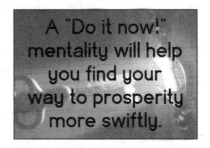

A "Do it now!" mentality will help you find your way to prosperity more swiftly.

Handling your finances with a *"Do it now!"* mentality will greatly assist you in finding your way to prosperity far more swiftly.

I have been told by well-meaning people that when they have a million dollars they will give a large sum to the church. My reply is that they should give what they have now. We often tend to postpone doing something if we are not truly committed to doing it in the first place. If we mean it, we'll do it—without delay, without fanfare. Just getting started on a task will put you well on your way to completing it.

"Tell me, what do you have in the house?" "Nothing at all, except a flask of olive oil," she replied.

(2 Kings 4:2 NLT)

Many people are waiting for that special day when they think they'll have more than they have now—and then they'll *really* be able to do something! However, they need to simply start *now* with whatever they've got.

When Elisha asked the woman what she had to repay the debts of her dead husband, she replied, "Nothing." Then she added that all she had was a small flask of oil. The prophet instructed her to get as many empty vessels together as she could and to start to use what she had by pouring it out. As she did, a miracle of provision began to flow. In fact, she was able to keep pouring until there were no more empty vessels! And that oil would have kept on pouring as long as she kept on supplying empty vessels.

Start with what you have, rather than thinking you have nothing and therefore can't start at all!

When our church began our television ministry, we only had two one-thousand-watt TV lights and one home video camera. But once we started filming, people began helping out with other equipment, and we soon found ourselves with three broadcast-quality cameras, proper lighting, and air-time on a regional channel reaching two hundred thousand people! As time has passed, we've found ourselves speaking to up to six hundred million people in a variety of different languages—all because we got started with what we had!

What do you have right now that you could start doing something with? Find it, and *do it now!*

KEY #29

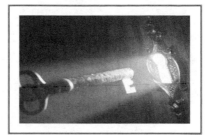

PROVISION FOR THE FAMILY

But if anyone does not provide for his own, and especially for those of his household, he has denied the faith and is worse than an unbeliever.
—1 Timothy 5:8

T he context of the Scripture above is that it is the responsibility of the church to care for widows. Paul gives Pastor Timothy some guidelines about who qualifies for financial assistance from the church. In the congregations at that time, there were many widows of soldiers who had died in the Roman wars. To ensure that the church would not be overly burdened with demand for financial support, Paul outlined in 1 Timothy 5:3–15 who could justifiably receive it.

The list is not lightweight:

✓ The qualifying woman spends night and day in prayer.

✓ She must be no less than sixty years old.

✓ She must have been faithful to her husband during their marriage.

✓ She must have been well respected.

✓ She must have raised her children well.

✓ She must have proven herself hospitable to strangers.

✓ She must have served other believers.

✓ She must have helped those in trouble.

✓ She must always have been ready to do good.

Even if a widow did not qualify at all points, if she had children or grandchildren, then they were to care for her, not the church! How often do you see that in today's church?

First Timothy 5:8 is often quoted in reference to husbands caring for their families. That is one correct application, of course, but the context is about children caring for their widowed mothers, so the church will not be burdened. People often see the church as a place for free handouts, even for those who're able to work. But the church is not meant to be a soft touch for the lazy. We should be teaching people how to build productive lives, rather than how to depend on charity. We need to encourage people to joyfully assume responsibility for their own lives and families; not complain about how little the government and church are helping.

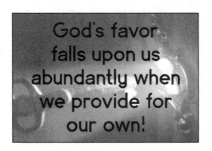

God's favor falls upon us abundantly when we provide for our own!

We live in a world where too many people avoid accepting responsibility. Taking responsibility is the path to building a successful life. In life, there is good pressure and bad pressure. Hard work is good pressure, because rather than seeking entertainment and pleasure, the hard worker seeks to be productive and responsible. Assuming responsibility for others—especially for our own family—is key to generating great income.

God's favor falls upon us abundantly when we provide for our own!

KEY #30

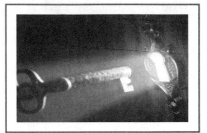

FAITHFULNESS IN MONEY

Therefore if you have not been faithful in the unrighteous mammon, who will commit to your trust the true riches?
—Luke 16:11

I n Luke 16, when Jesus established by what criteria faithfulness is judged, He pointed to three areas:

1. Little things
2. Money
3. What belongs to others

He revealed that if we've been faithful in those areas, then we qualify to be given great responsibility, true riches, and our own world to rule over!

I would have thought that if I prove to be faithful with spiritual riches, then God would release to me worldly riches. Yet, exactly the opposite is true: He watches to see if we pay our bills and if we are honest and diligent in dealing with small amounts of money. It constantly amazes me how much goodwill is established when we are reliable with money and unconditionally generous. When we prove ourselves responsible at one level of finances, He then moves us up to the next level.

I recall one day when I was buying some food at a Greek shop and the price came to around thirty-seven dollars. I paid the owner forty dollars and told him to keep the change. He tried to give me back the change. I refused. He stopped what he was doing and called out for his mother, his brother, and his children to all come, and he told them what I had done. It was only three dollars, yet this man was celebrating! They gave me bottles of sauce off the shelf that amounted to much more than

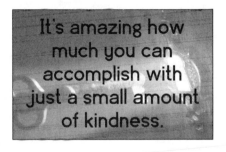

three dollars. Their view of the pastor was greatly enhanced just because of a few bucks!

It is amazing how much you can accomplish with just a small amount of kindness.

Another time I was buying some meat at a butcher shop. I picked out some bones for the dog, which added only two more dollars to the cost. But I had run out of money, so the butcher told me to bring it in next time. I knew I might forget because it was such a small amount. So I went home, got two dollars, and came right back with it. Even though it was a tiny amount, he remembered that the pastor pays his bills! If he ever hears others speak ill of me, he'll tell them, "Well, all I know is the guy pays his bills!" If I had forgotten and never paid even that small amount back, the pastor's reputation would have been just the opposite!

―――――◆―――――

Faithfulness is about *living right with God's money!* When we do that, Jesus will entrust us with true revelation from the Word of God. We should make right any financial areas that are wrong in our lives—the desire to please God alone should motivate us to do that. But God Himself promises that if we are faithful with money, then He will bless us with even greater riches!

KEY #31

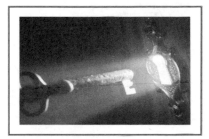

FINANCIAL PLANNING MAXIMIZES YOUR RESOURCES

We should make plans—counting on God to direct us.
—Proverbs 16:9 TLB

Without a plan, money disappears. Without a plan, money does not appear. Without a plan, a goal or a vision, you will not manage your money well, nor will you ever maximize its value.

A financial plan begins with identifying what you want to achieve. Answer the following questions, and you're at the starting point of a financial plan:

✓ *How much are you going to earn this year, next year, and ten years from now?*

✓ *When do you plan to pay off your house?*

✓ *Are you going to have enough to retire with an abundance? How much is that?*

✓ *When will you be completely out of debt?*

✓ *How many houses do you plan to own?*

✓ *What inheritance do you want to leave your children?*

✓ *How much money do you plan to give to God and others in your lifetime?*

As you answer these questions and others you may think of, you will establish your vision, goals, and a plan to achieve them.

Anybody planning on earning money needs to sit down and decide how they are going to generate that money and then decide what they are going to do with that money. Otherwise it will simply—pfft!—go away...and often with us having no idea where it went.

A Budget Is a Powerful Tool!

Be diligent to know the state of your flocks, and attend to your herds; for riches are not forever.
(Proverbs 27:23–24)

A budget may sound boring, but it is actually a powerful tool to live by. Your budget reflects your priorities and values. What you believe in, the principles you live by, and the things that are important to you should be budgeted as your top priorities.

We all know people who list the things that are important to them, yet they fail to give financial priority to those items. That is indicative of a lack of financial discipline. Financial discipline begins with a *budget!*

Principles of Productivity

If we say that God is first in our life, then He should get the first of our finances.

If we declare that our family is important, then they should get the lion's share of the budget in housing, clothing, schooling, and vacations.

Let me describe the simplest of budgets. Take a piece of paper and, on the left side, list all of the income you receive from all sources. Add it up, placing the total at the bottom of the page. On the right-hand side of the page, list all of your expenses. Put your tithes at the top (which will equal 10 percent of the total on the left-hand side). Then list your taxes, rent or home loan repayments, food bill, all utilities (water, electricity, phone), clothes and extras, and your investments. Whatever is leftover is for nonessentials, such as entertainment.

———

Here is a simple young wage-earner's weekly budget:

Income:		Outgo:	
Wages	750	Tithe	75
Interest	20	Taxes	200
		Home loan	200
		Food	125
		Utilities	70
		Investment/savings	30
		Clothes/extras	40
		Entertainment	30
Total Income:	**770**	**Total Outgo:**	**770**

Each week, keep yourself strictly to that list. If you develop this skill early in your financial life, you'll find that it guides you as you run businesses and large organizations and deal with millions. As you begin investing in shares and properties, you'll have a skill that will enable you to decide how you will continually increase your income. If you have no plan for your money, then it will disappear, and after years of working hard, you will have nothing to show for it.

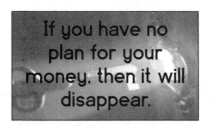

If you have no plan for your money, then it will disappear.

KEY #32

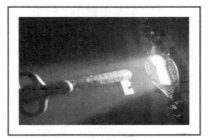

SOUND BUSINESS PRACTICES LEAD TO SOLID SUCCESS

Be diligent to know the state of your flocks, and attend to your herds.
—Proverbs 27:23

I t is vital to always be aware of the exact circumstances of your personal finances, the state of the various sources that bring money into your life. It is equally vital to know what you are spending your money on. Unrestrained spending breeds doom! Everyone has spending limits. It's imperative to know what yours are and to remain within those limits. Otherwise, unmanageable debt will consume your prosperity.

If you manage your personal finances well, you will be able to translate those disciplines and skills into your businesses and all other organizations you have a hand in.

People unaware of the financial numbers in their organization are simply flying blind. Even though I lead a church and direct an international movement of churches, I am also involved in overseeing a school of one thousand children and over one hundred employees. I oversee three colleges that train people in ministry, the arts, and counseling. We run a television studio, a bookshop, a recording label, and a café. All of these are businesses with employees, products, and services, and all require management and leadership to remain healthy and productive. These businesses generate millions of dollars annually. It is impossible to think that we can run these enterprises without knowing the financial numbers. There must be current records of everything, from cash flow to inventory, from overhead to net profits, from client database to quality controls. There are hundreds of crucial items that require detailed attention on a daily basis.

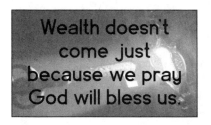

Wealth doesn't come just because we pray God will bless us.

Wealth doesn't come just because we pray that God will bless us. All too often, many Christians are naïve, and they imagine that God is just going to bless them—even when they ignore all the basics of running a business!

I often speak at Christian business events. There are always great people in these meetings. However, it is astonishing how many have tried and failed, and how many experience ongoing tough times. Most have found that their tough times are due to bad business practices, and not attacks from the devil. Some think that if they are convinced their business idea is from God, then it will automatically be blessed. I have news for you: There is a *lot* more to being successful than just having a good idea! There are thousands of good ideas that never make it, all because of a lack of good management. And there are some very average products and services that have become quite successful because they have been managed very well.

In Australia, for every one hundred business start-ups only four are still operating after ten years!

Anyone who runs a business must have at least a basic training in bookkeeping and learn how to analyze the numbers and how to operate the vast array of different ingredients that go into making a business successful. Learning sound business practices is crucial if you want to enjoy solid success in your financial endeavors.

KEY #33

DEBT CANCELLATION

*At the end of every seven years you shall
grant a release of debts.*
—Deuteronomy 15:1

D ebt is a heavy bondage for most people in today's
world. But God wants us set free from it, and He has
enabled us to do just that. Throughout Scripture we
learn that God works at releasing people from the bondage
of their debts.

According to statistics, credit card debt is now the
number one reason stated for bankruptcy filings.[1] From
2000 to 2004, cases of bankruptcy shot up by over 28 percent, to 1,635,725 cases nationally.[2] Last year, 98 percent
of all insolvencies were caused by personal financial lia-
bilities—credit cards, mobile phones, personal loans, and
other credit.[3] And here's the stunning part: In Australia,

---

[1] http://www.bankruptcyhome.com/top10reasons.htm

[2] http://www.bankruptcyaction.com/USbankstats.htm#bankruptcyprofile

[3] http://www.bna.com/webwatch/bankruptcycrs3.pdf

two-thirds of people filing for bankruptcy have debts of less than $20,000.

People are trying to get out of debt by simply declaring themselves insolvent and unable to repay their obligations. But the quick-fix of bankruptcy has a serious downside: The action remains on your credit profile for seven years, preventing you from obtaining a loan or a credit card or even renting property. Also, a permanent record is on file in the federal court where the bankruptcy was granted.

A Culture of Debt

Money problems are a leading cause of anxiety, depression, and sleeplessness. Financial struggles are at the root of a multitude of family and friendship breakdowns, due to lack of money or loans going unpaid.[4] Statistics reveal that money trouble is the leading cause of divorce. And citizens of the Western democracies tend to have the lowest savings percentage rate in the entire world; yet, it is commonplace for people to spend more than they earn!

Because governments have adopted a borrowing lifestyle, rather than learning to be more income-generating, nearly one-third of our lives is spent working to pay taxes to the government. In America, April 15 is an appropriate federal income tax filing deadline, because most people's income up to that date goes to the government. As if that weren't bad enough, people spend another 60 percent of their working lives paying off money they have borrowed.

---

[4] A. Vinokur, R. Price, R. Caplan, "Hard Times and Hurtful Partners: How Financial Strain Affects Depression and Relationship Satisfaction of Unemployed Persons and Their Spouses," *Journal of Peronsality and Social Psychology* 71, no. 1 (1996): 166–179, http://www.isr.umich.edu/src/seh/mprc/PDFs/Vin_jpsp96.pdf

We have developed a culture of debt that has become the norm. The Bible refers to those who have to borrow money as "the poor," but regards you as blessed and wealthy when you own everything you live in, drive in, and work in, and owe nobody anything, but rather are in a position to lend and to give to others.

I have no problem with manageable, justifiable borrowing. However, I'd rather put money into paying off a mortgage than into rent, for example. Rents continually go up, whereas mortgage payments generally decrease over time. And with mortgages, you're putting money into your own pocket by paying down the loan and increasing your equity. Whereas with renting, you're putting money into someone else's pocket with no hope of an equity return.

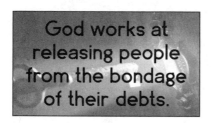

God works at releasing people from the bondage of their debts.

In April 1988, the magazine *Christian Retailing* revealed that the average charismatic Christian in America spends a total of just $2.17 per week on everything Christian, including offerings. So, while we put a large part of our money into interest and borrowings, we have become completely unable to be full partners with God in the greatest project in all the earth: Building His church and winning the lost to Christ!

Often, with the challenge of having to cover all the bills, it can seem impossible to pay even that 10 percent sliver of a tithe, let alone to bring an offering and make a commitment to missions. Many Christians feel hopeless about their finances.

They feel they are in an endless stream of borrowing, where unpaid bills occupy more and more of their thoughts. They have lost hope that there is any way out of debt. These are not "bad" people; they are hardworking, honest people who are trying their best to simply make ends meet. But there are things they need to focus on doing better—in God's ways, not man's ways.

God is as concerned about your financial success as He is about the health of your body, the happiness of your relationships, and the success of your entire life.

God's Ways

In Israel, the people were able to take a year off from repaying their debts every seven years. Furthermore, in the year of Jubilee (every fifty years), all debts were cancelled, all land that had been sold because of financial pressure had to be returned to the original owner, and all slaves were set free!

Not only had God prescribed laws that eliminated debt, but when His people found themselves dealing with unmanageable debt, He moved to help to release them through miraculous means. In fact, the entire point of the death of Jesus was to pay a debt that we owed to the justice of God. The only payment that was acceptable for our sins was our death, but God decided to pay that debt if we would simply repent and receive His Son.

God's Release

A certain woman of the wives of the sons of the prophets cried out to Elisha, saying, "Your servant my husband is dead, and you know that your servant feared the LORD. And the creditor is coming to take my two sons to be his slaves." So Elisha said to her, "What shall I do for you? Tell me, what do you have in the house?" And she said, "Your maidservant has nothing in the house but a jar of oil." Then he said, "Go, borrow vessels from everywhere, from all your neighbors—empty vessels; do not gather just a few. And when you have come in, you shall shut the door behind you and your sons; then pour it into all those vessels, and set aside the full ones." So she went from him and shut the door behind her and her sons, who brought the vessels to her; and she poured it out. Now it came to pass, when the vessels were full, that she said to her son, "Bring me another vessel." And he said to her, "There is not another vessel." So the oil ceased.   (2 Kings 4:1–6)

The story in 2 Kings is one of the great stories of the power and mercy of God to release a person from one of the worst situations in life:

> One of the young men training in the school of the prophets had decided to take out a large loan, possibly to purchase a home. He loved God and had given his life to serve Him. His wife and children loved God. The entire family had consecrated themselves to God for a life in ministry. But then, the most unbelievable thing happens: The young man dies. His beautiful young wife is left penniless to look after her two boys and to service the loan as well. The creditor is merciless. The widow didn't have enough equity to cover the entire debt. So, as was legal and acceptable in that time, the creditor went

to the woman to claim her two sons as his slaves to sell in order to recover his money! The mother is devastated, utterly helpless, and completely vulnerable.

When we are faced with problems like these, we can become angry with God. Sometimes we can't understand why such terrible things can happen when we are serving God. But a problem is simply an opportunity for a miracle.

This woman doesn't run from God, she ran *to* Him. The prophet Elisha has mercy on her. He doesn't take advantage of her problem or use it as an opportunity to chastise her for getting into this state of affairs.

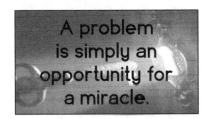

A problem is simply an opportunity for a miracle.

It's a sad day when people in trouble seek help only to find rebuke. Too many ministers accuse people of misdeeds when they are experiencing problems in their lives. The world is full of Job counselors, when what is needed is people who will help ease the problem, not make it worse.

The woman not only hears what Elisha told her to do, she actually does it. He asks her what she has in the house. She has nothing. Everything has been sold to try to satisfy the creditor. All she has left is a small bottle of oil. God can do anything with whatever we have—and that oil was more than enough! The prophet tells her to make herself ready to receive an incredible miracle. She borrows every empty vessel she can to receive the miraculous provision of God...and He pours it on!

Look to God Alone!

How often it is that we need a disaster in order to get desperate enough to get before God in trust and obedience. God's miracle would have been available to the couple before they borrowed the money. But they looked to *man* for their provision first, instead of God. Yet, when repayment became impossible, then the woman looked to God.

We should look to God from the very outset of every endeavor. The miracles of God always meet our needs. They are practical. They are not an end in themselves. The woman wasn't to store the oil as some religious artifact. She was to sell it, make enough profit for her to pay off the debt, and then live for the rest of her days off what was left over. Her greatest problem became her greatest blessing because, in faith, she made a decision to pour out all she had left, in spite of the huge challenge she faced! And God came through, as He always does when we reach to Him in faith.

God supplies abundance. Out of that woman's worst circumstances, God provided the best days of her life. She would never have to work again. All she needed to do was raise the boys on the income God had given her. The Lord had not only solved the most difficult problem she had ever faced, but He also became her provider, replacing the husband she had lost.

Pay all your debts, except the debt of love for others. You can never finish paying that! (Romans 13:8 NLT)

The miracles of God release us from debt. However, without the desire or a plan to be out of debt, the power of God will *not* assist us. Our will is what God moves through. If we discipline our spending and work at generating income and paying off our debts, then God will help us to achieve exactly that.

James Moffatt once said, "A man's treatment of money is the most decisive test of his character—how he makes it and how he spends it."

In *Hamlet,* even Shakespeare lectured against debt:

> Costly thy habit as thy purse can buy, but not express'd in fancy; rich, not gaudy; for the apparel oft proclaims the man, and they in France of the best rank and station are most select and generous, chief in that. Neither a borrower nor a lender be; for a loan oft loses both itself and friend, and borrowing dulls the edge of husbandry. This above all: to thine own self be true, and it must follow, as the night the day, thou canst not then be false to any man.[5]

Make the commitment right now to be out of debt! Imagine how amazing it would be to have no debts at all. Imagine how amazing it would be to owe nobody, no bank, no business, no loaning institution, a single penny. Imagine how amazing it would be to have money in your account that you could give or loan to anyone at any time they need it. Imagine how amazing it would be to give not just tithes but also great offerings to God and His work in the earth.

These imaginings will become reality if you will apply discipline to your spending to get yourself out of debt so you may buy those things you need and pay your rent and bills before using your money for anything else.

---

[5] William Shakespeare, *Hamlet*, 1.3.74–84.

There are many things people think they need but can honestly do without. Make a list of all the things you spend money on. Determine which of those you can do without. Be ruthless in reducing your spending so you can get out of debt and stay out of it. Discipline is not something we hear a lot about; but without it, all of our dreams will flounder and die.

If you have a large number of debts, then you are better off consolidating them into one loan to pay off as soon as possible. If those debts are credit cards, then get rid of all but one, so you won't have access to cash you can't afford.

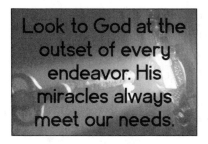

Look to God at the outset of every endeavor. His miracles always meet our needs.

Money is powerful. It needs strong management. It demands discipline if it is to be a blessing to us and to others. If we are always in debt, then we may not be able to help others—and we are often paying for things more than twice over because of interest rates.

Jesus announced that He had come to proclaim the year of Jubilee. That was the year when all debts were to be cancelled in Israel. Everyone got a fresh start once a lifetime. Accept that promise from heaven and begin working today on building a debt-free lifestyle, knowing that the promise of God *will* assist you!

KEY #34

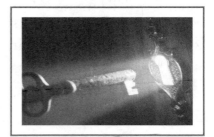

GOD'S POWER IN GAINING WEALTH

And you shall remember the LORD your God, for it is
He who gives you power to get wealth.
—Deuteronomy 8:18

T he *New Living Translation* of the Scripture above says
that it is God who gives us power to become *"rich."*

The Lord has not promised that every believer will
become wealthy. He says that He will give you *"power to get
wealth."* He does not say that He will give you wealth. But He
has promised that all those who have entered into the new
covenant with Him through Christ will have opportunity to
prosper. We all have been given the ability, if we will harness
it, to generate finances. There is an enormous variety of ways
for money to come into our hands. The way we invest our
time, skill, experience, and knowledge should be guided by
God so we have the possibility of gaining maximum return.

Passive Income

The term *passive income* is one of the most powerful concepts that can guide us into lives of prosperity. The person who is locked into the thinking of a salaried career will always have a lid on his possibilities of prospering.

We Christians have been seriously handicapped in our mind-set with regard to prospering in life. Therefore, we have not allowed ourselves to think even mildly creatively about how to generate vast sums of money. The Protestant work ethic—great and essential as it is—can also be severely restrictive. We should definitely work hard; but working hard is not all there is to making money. What we need is to work *smart*.

———◆———

Most education for work or career is aimed at equipping people with the skills and knowledge to get a job that they can be paid to work at. There are virtually no courses in education that teach people how to make money in ways other than career performance.

Here are the four ascending levels of income:

1. **Time and labor**: You give an employer eight working hours of each day at physical labor (standing at a cashier, digging holes, driving a truck, etc.), and get paid an agreed rate for that time.

2. **Skill**: You develop skills that an employer pays you to use to get a job done. You can fix a motor, so you get paid an agreed amount to do that job, regardless of how long it takes you. You can charge more for this than a person just getting a time-based income.

3. **Wisdom**: You learn how to arrange for motors to be fixed, the shop to be run, the fleet of cars to be organized, and you are able to consult, manage, and oversee a team of employees to perform these various tasks. Your knowledge in that area is worth a higher level of money. People who don't know what you know can waste money, time, and resources before they are able to fix the problem. Because you do know, the problem is solved quickly and the goals achieved easily; thus, your input is valued at a higher rate.

4. **Passive income**: This is the area of greatest opportunity for the generation of unlimited income. If we can step into this area, then God is able to provide great opportunities through which abundance can flow into our lives. Passive income is where we take the money we have earned through any of the previously mentioned means—time and labor, skill, or wisdom—and we buy something that generates income without us having to do anything except a bit of minor administrating. This means buying stock shares that keep increasing in value and generating income at the same time. This means buying rental properties that people pay to live in. In fact, stock and real estate represent the two most common forms of passive income.

We would serve ourselves well to become educated in an area we feel comfortable with and then work out a plan to earn passive income from that involvement. Seek out people who have been successful with passive investing and ask them questions. Read books by people who have proven track records dealing with passive income. Educate yourself!

There are many areas that can bring passive income your way: Royalties from songs or books, inventions you have acquired, stocks and bonds, and many others.

Let me simplify the concept by referring to just one area: Real estate. Most people have equity in their own home that simply sits there year after year, never being used. That's called lazy money, or "house banking." Most banks are willing, if not eager, to loan money against that equity. If you have exercised due diligence in finding a property that has great rental return plus capital growth, then you can approach a lender with confidence about your project. Ask others who have been successful in the same area about their thoughts on the probable income and output of the project. If you can get started on a small project, then you will gain knowledge and experience at a lower risk.

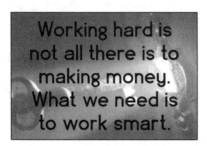

Working hard is not all there is to making money. What we need is to work smart.

Be patient, not greedy. Enduring wealth never comes quickly; nor is it necessary to take enormous risks. Don't place your entire home at risk. Borrow a small percentage of the equity at first. The goal should always be to pay down the mortgages as soon as possible. Once the property is unencumbered, it is a genuine asset that claims no capital from us, but instead pays money to us. As time passes, equity builds in the properties we purchase so we are able to borrow more against our equity in order to purchase more. As we sleep, people are paying us rent. That is called *passive income*.

In our church, we teach young people about the creation of passive income. Consequently, young adults in their twenties own entire apartment complexes and have become millionaires. The sooner young people understand how to generate, manage, and distribute wealth, the more blessing they can be in this world.

I wish I had attended a church like ours when I was young. I only began later in life to believe it was possible for a Christian to enjoy financial wealth. Starting late in life is better than nothing, but how much better to have been able to do this as a younger person! One of the greatest joys I know is paying a family's medical bills for their child's operation, paying someone's rent when he loses his job, and buying a single mother a car. That is what Christians should be able to do. However, many are so bound up in an anti-wealth mind-set that the church has been severely constrained from being much of a blessing to the world at all.

KEY #35

TIMING, PATIENCE, AND THE CREATION OF WEALTH

Prepare your outside work, make it fit for yourself in the field; and afterward build your house.
—Proverbs 24:27

P roverbs 24:27 instructs you to prepare the ground, plant the seed, and get ready for the harvest before building your house. If you spend all your energy and money building your house without looking after the farm first, then you'll have no harvest in the summer to pay for the house.

This is about *patience*. It's about getting an income established and getting what you need before you start pursuing the things you want.

At Christian City Church, we plant many other churches. One of the basics for young pastors starting a church is to first get the church going, then buy a house. My wife and I both worked in the business world at the start of our church, so the young church wasn't burdened with our salaries. After six months, though, I left the insurance industry and Chris left her sales job, because we needed to commit more time to the growing church and the budget could now afford to pay a wage. We lived in rented houses for three years, then finally bought a house for the family.

If a young pastor commits himself to a mortgage before the church has really got going, he will find himself under unnecessary pressure to raise money, not just for the church, but also to pay off his house. This confuses his motivation and inhibits church growth.

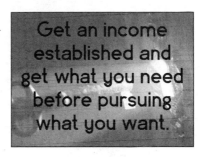

Get an income established and get what you need before pursuing what you want.

I've seen people with great ideas leave their job to devote all their time and savings on getting their ideas up and running. However, there are very few people who can achieve this. We should arrange our world to meet our needs, rather than trying to fulfill our dreams. Once we have the basics covered, we can fully devote ourselves to developing our dreams. People are far wiser when they keep a steady income and "moonlight" their idea. No matter how great the idea is, it will always take time before it generates income. People need to eat and sleep somewhere while their ideas get off the ground. They can work at night and on weekends, every spare moment, getting the project going. They don't have to watch TV, read magazines, eat out at restaurants, etc.

The launching of any great project involves wise timing, sacrifice in the early days of the birthing, and patience.

REASONS TO GIVE SACRIFICIAL OFFERINGS TO GOD

KEY #36

REASON ONE:
THE POWER OF TESTIMONY

*Moreover, brethren, we make known to you the
grace of God bestowed on the* [five] *churches of
Macedonia* [Phillipi, Nicopolis, Thessalonica, Appolonia
and Berea]: *that in a great trial of affliction the
abundance of their joy and their deep poverty
abounded in the riches of their liberality. For I
bear witness that according to their ability, yes,
and beyond their ability, they were freely willing,
imploring us with much urgency that we would
receive the gift and the fellowship of the ministering
to the saints. And not only as we had hoped, but they
first gave themselves to the Lord, and then to us by
the will of God. So we urged Titus, that as he had
begun, so he would also complete this
grace in you as well.*
—2 Corinthians 8:1–6

REASONS TO GIVE SACRIFICIAL OFFERINGS TO GOD

I n the passage above, Paul has a project. He has traveled around to churches and raised pledges from them for the poor Jerusalem church. Corinth was wealthy; Macedonia was poor. Paul provokes the wealthy Corinthians not to be outdone in their giving by the poor Macedonians.

People throughout the world give to the Lord in extraordinary ways. Within local congregations it is well-known that not everybody gives. Some give with deep sacrifice; others with little sacrifice at all. Some give occasionally; others give regularly. Paul urges that there no longer be such inequality of giving among the people of God, but that everyone assume responsibility in giving.

In Portugal, Pastor Jorge Tadeu, leader of the Mana churches, told the people that if they are not tithing, then they are not welcome in the church. This is not a small church, either. It is a church of thousands of people. Pastor Tadeu under- 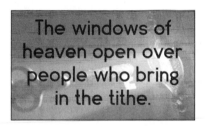 stands that we have a corporate responsibility to ensure that the blessing of God rests upon a congregation.

The book of Malachi reveals that the windows of heaven open over people who bring in the tithe. This means the windows of heaven are closed over people who are not bringing the tithe into the house of God.

Every one of us needs to be giving, rather than just leaving it to a few to carry the burden. Being a believer means that we learn to accept responsibility for the blessing of God resting not just on our own lives but on the lives of all those around us.

Using the Corinthians as a testimony to stir up the other churches, Paul boasted of their large pledges and their eagerness to be involved in the project of the service to the saints:

> There is no need for me to write to you about this service to the saints. For I know your eagerness to help, and I have been boasting about it to the Macedonians, telling them that since last year you in Achaia were ready to give; and your enthusiasm has stirred most of them to action. But I am sending the brothers in order that our boasting about you in this matter should not prove hollow, but that you may be ready, as I said you would be. For if any Macedonians come with me and find you unprepared, we—not to say anything about you—would be ashamed of having been so confident. So I thought it necessary to urge the brothers to visit you in advance and finish the arrangements for the generous gift you had promised. Then it will be ready as a generous gift, not as one grudgingly given.   (2 Corinthians 9:1–5 NIV)

One great reason for us to give is the fact that we are standing before a God who has received offerings from thousands of people throughout all the earth. We must be stirred by the giving of others. When we understand how much other people have given throughout the ages, as well as in our own times, we will be moved to give more, especially when those people are our friends or members of our own church.

I always ask people to testify when they have received blessing from heaven after having given to God. The testimony of others stirs people to greater levels of giving and receiving.

KEY #37

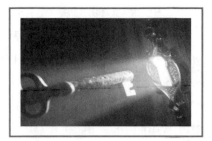

REASON TWO:
THE RESPONSIBILITY
OF LEADERSHIP

*But as you abound in everything; in faith, in speech,
in knowledge, in all diligence, and in your love for us;
see that you abound in this grace also. I speak not by
commandment, but I am testing the sincerity of your
love by the diligence of others.*
—2 Corinthians 8:7–8

The Corinthian church was enjoying an abundance of spiritual gifts and progress in every area of church life. The Corinthians had been leaders in many areas of church life, and now Paul tells them they need to become leaders in the realm of giving, as well.

Whenever a group has been blessed in any area, it is incumbent upon them to be generous with that success.

In monetary terms, most areas of spiritual gift ministry cost very little. In fact, most people are eager to heal the sick, work miracles, prophesy, or speak in tongues because those gifts help us feel that we have gained some ground in God. That is an exciting part of the adventure of being in Christ.

However, *giving* is another matter. I don't know of anyone who has fasted for forty days to receive the gift of giving. Giving is a gift that will financially cost us. It involves sacrifice and faith.

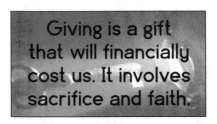

Giving is a gift that will financially cost us. It involves sacrifice and faith.

In 2 Corinthians 8, Paul appeals to the Corinthians to show that they are genuinely spiritual people by displaying not only their spiritual gifts, but also their generosity of spirit. *Generosity* is what shows that we are filled with the Holy Spirit.

Any leadership church that functions in an apostolic role must also assume the responsibility of leadership in the area of generous giving, so that others might follow the example.

At our church, whenever we have interviewed people to take a position on our building fund committee, we let them know that because it is a leadership role, their level of giving will need to be at a leadership level. People follow leaders. The responsibility of leadership means that we must do things that inspire others to go higher than they would have gone without our influence.

I recently attended a board meeting of our school. We were discussing how to raise funds for a new $3.3 million assembly hall. As we discussed different ways of raising the finances, I announced that everyone in the room needed to consider giving at a leadership level. Most of the board members are business people. One member is the school's headmaster, and two others are pastors. I made a commitment to contribute $5,000. I said that if I, being just a pastor, could give that much, then imagine what the others could do. By the end of that meeting, we had raised over $100,000—and that was just the school board, it wasn't even the building fund committee from whom we could expect far higher sums! Because we were members of the school board, we had to act like leaders in order to influence others to step up as well.

———————

Whether or not you are involved in leadership, you are involved in influencing others. People base their actions in this life on the way others act—particularly those they respect. We are all involved in making disciples—which is leading others to Christ. Thus, as leaders, we need to act like it at all times. As leaders set the example of giving, others will follow.

Key #38

Reason Three:
The Example of Christ

For you know the grace of our Lord Jesus Christ, that though He was rich, yet for your sakes He became poor, that you through His poverty might become rich.
—2 Corinthians 8:9

I n the Scripture above, Paul appeals to the fact that Jesus, though rich, gave up everything for us. It is important to understand the time frame this verse refers to. Most people believe it refers to when Jesus left heaven to come to earth, inferring that He was rich in heaven and became poor when He came to earth. That is actually not an accurate inference. Scripture shows that Christ had access to great wealth while on earth. Furthermore, because Jesus lived a life that fulfilled all the requirements of the law of Moses, He inherited all the promised blessings of the Mosaic law. If we believe He was poor during his life on earth, we are saying that He was living under the curse that Moses pronounced on those who were disobedient to the Law. We would also then have to conclude that though Jesus was healthy in heaven, He became sick on earth.

With very little inspection, this point of view quickly disintegrates.

The fact is, the Scripture refers to when Christ went to the cross. It was there that He became sin for our sin (2 Corinthians 5:21), sick with our sicknesses (1 Peter 2:24), and poor with our poverty (2 Corinthians 8:9). Yet, all along, He had access to everything on earth, for He made *everything*—and it all belongs to Him!

> *Through him all things were made; without him nothing was made that has been made.*
>
> (John 1:3 NIV)

KEY #39

REASON FOUR:
INTEGRITY OF PROMISE

And in this I give advice: It is to your advantage not only to be doing what you began and were desiring to do a year ago; but now you also must complete the doing of it; that as there was a readiness to desire it, so there also may be a completion out of what you have.
—2 Corinthians 8:10–11

In the passage above, Paul appeals to the integrity of the Corinthians, that they would not go back on their word. The Corinthians had pledged to give a certain amount. They had given some, but not all of it; and now Paul is urging them to complete what they began.

The reason many believers have such a hard time believing the Word of God is because they don't believe their own word. Somewhere inside of them they know they don't really have any intention of keeping what they promise. When we make a promise, we must realize how important it is to keep it. It's a matter of our integrity as Christians and the example that we put out to the world.

Making pledges is part of the Christian life. A pledge is another word for *commitment*. For some people, the word commitment is the "C" word—they're terrified by it because they're suddenly locked into having to do something. Their options have narrowed. There's no back door. However, *nothing* is achieved without commitment!

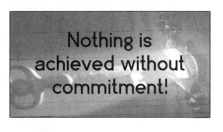

Nothing is achieved without commitment!

One of the best commitment statements I've come across is this one from Pastor Bob Moorhead:

I, [your name here] am part of the "Fellowship of the Unashamed." The die has been cast. The decision has been made. I have stepped over the line. I won't look back, let up, slow down, back away, or be still.

My past is redeemed, my present makes sense, and my future is secure. I'm finished and done with low living, slight walking, small planning, smooth knees, colorless dreams, tamed visions, mundane talking, cheap giving, and dwarfed goals.

I no longer need preeminence, prosperity, position, promotions, plaudits, or popularity. I don't have to be right, first, tops, recognized, praised, regarded, or rewarded. I now live by faith, lean on His presence, love with patience, live by prayer, and labor with power.

My face is set, my gait is fast, my goal is heaven, my road is narrow, my way is rough, my companions are few, my Guide is reliable, and my mission is clear. I cannot be bought, compromised, detoured, lured away, turned back, deluded, or delayed. I will not flinch in the face of sacrifice, hesitate in the presence of adversity, negotiate at the table of the enemy, ponder at the pool of popularity, or meander in the maze of mediocrity.

I won't give up, shut up, let up, or slow up until I have stayed up, stored up, prayed up, paid up, and spoken up for the cause of Christ. I am a disciple of Jesus. I must go till He comes, give till I drop, preach till all know, and work till He stops me.

And when Jesus comes for His own, He will have no problem recognizing me. My banner is clear: I am a part of the "Fellowship of the Unashamed."

A pastor of one of the largest churches in Southern California says, "Unfortunately, churches are often held together by committees rather than by commitment."

It is not possible to be "committed" without some actual project or event to be committed to. Our commitment needs a specific project, an actual context, in order to be real. When it comes to financial projects, we should make a pledge, and then fulfill that commitment. Standing by our word is what builds character and generosity into our lives. The basis of character, integrity, and trustworthiness is that we will *keep our word*. The basis for all of our faith and trust in God is that we know that He will keep His Word and commitments and will always do what He says. If God were not to keep His Word, the entire universe would fail!

Everything is held together by the power of God's Word (2 Peter 3:7).

Commitment: The Power of the Vow

Then Jacob made a vow, saying, "If God will be with me, and keep me in this way that I am going, and give me bread to eat and clothing to put on, so that I come back to my father's house in peace, then the LORD shall be my God. And this stone which I have set as a pillar shall be God's house, and of all that You give me I will surely give a tenth to You."

(Genesis 28:20–22)

The word *commitment* is not found in Scripture. However, the concept of commitment is in the use of the words *vow* and *pledge*. Vows are commitments to action that we make to God and that we intend to fulfill.

God makes promises, commitments, and vows. People make promises back to God. Vows have been a normal part of life with God since the beginning. *Vow* is translated from the Hebrew word *nedar*, which means "to promise." The Greek for vow is *euche*, which means "a prayer."

Genesis 28:18–22 tells the story of how Jacob came to make a vow to God to give Him a tenth of all his possessions. He has left his home to go to Haran, the same place where, generations before, God had spoken to Abram about the land the Hebrews would one day possess. On the way, Jacob stops at Bethel ("House of God"), where Abram had built an altar to God (Genesis 12:8). Jacob takes a stone (not inconceivably one of the stones from Abram's altar) to use as a pillow.

He falls asleep...and has a dream. God meets with Jacob in a dream in the night. The following morning, Jacob makes an altar of the stone, pours oil on it, consecrates himself to the Lord, and commits to God to give Him a tenth of all that God gives him from that day forward. All that Jacob committed himself to doing, he did; and all that God said He would do, He did.

The Vow of Hannah

> *Then* [Hannah] *made a vow and said, "O LORD of hosts, if You will indeed look on the affliction of Your maidservant and remember me, and not forget Your maidservant, but will give Your maidservant a male child, then I will give him to the LORD all the days of his life, and no razor shall come upon his head."*
>
> (1 Samuel 1:11)

As a result of this prayer, Hannah conceives and brings forth a child named Samuel. Then she carries out her vow to God by giving Him the boy. Samuel grows to become one of the most significant and powerful prophets in all of history.

David's Vow to God

> *LORD, remember David and all his afflictions; How he swore to the LORD, and vowed to the Mighty One of Jacob: "Surely I will not go into the chamber of my house, or go up to the comfort of my bed; I will not give sleep to my eyes or slumber to my eyelids, until I find a place for the LORD, a dwelling place for the Mighty One of Jacob."* (Psalm 132:1–5)

Vows are made freely throughout the Bible. No one is forced to make them. God never demanded of us, "Thou shalt vow to do thus and such!" It is the worshipper who makes the pledge voluntarily and with a free spirit.

———◆———

The Bible gives us clear instructions about how vows are to be made:

1. **With a cheerful attitude**. 2 Corinthians 9:7: *"For God loves a cheerful giver."*

2. **Freely, without constraint, willingly, and not under compulsion**. 2 Corinthians 9:7: *"So let each one give as he purposes in his heart, not grudgingly or of necessity."*

3. **Only that which we know we can follow through on**. We are to commit to give what we have, not what we do not have. 2 Corinthians 8:12: *"For if there is first a willing mind, it is accepted according to what one has, and not according to what he does not have."* We should base our giving on our known income, plus any other sources or assets we are able to give from.

4. **As an ongoing activity throughout our lives**. We should arrange to give regularly, and start immediately. 1 Corinthians 16:2: *"On the first day of the week let each one of you lay something aside, storing up as he may prosper."*

People who give regularly, and begin as soon as possible, are most successful in accomplishing their commitment to God.

I suggest arranging direct debits from your bank account to your church, mission, and other places you commit to give to, as a convenient way to carry through with your vows without hesitation or the possibility of distraction through outside temptation.

Fulfilling Your Commitment

Here are some important guidelines in carrying out your promises and commitments concerning gifts, tithes, ministry support, and other financial vows you make:

1. **Do not delay in fulfilling your commitment**. Once you are able to fulfill it, do it right away. Deuteronomy 23:21, emphasis added: *"When you make a vow to the LORD your God, **you shall not delay to pay it**; for the LORD your God will surely require it of you, and it would be sin to you."* Ecclesiastes 5:4–6, emphasis added: *"When you make a vow to God, **do not delay to pay it**; for He has no pleasure in fools. Pay what you have vowed: Better not to vow than to vow and not pay. Do not let your mouth cause your flesh to sin, nor say before the messenger of God that it was an error. Why should God be angry at your excuse and destroy the work of your hands?"*

2. **Don't be hasty or rash in vow-making**. Take time. Seek counsel. Be wise. Proverbs 20:25: *"It is a snare for a man to devote rashly something as holy, and afterward to reconsider his vows."*

3. **Don't use for yourself what you have vowed to give to God,** for it is devoted to the Lord. Proverbs 20:25 KJV: *"It is a snare to the man who devoureth that which is holy, and after vows to make inquiry."*

4. **Protect your offering**. Sacrifices and offerings are powerful. Satan will attempt to destroy them or prevent us from carrying them through because of the blessing it releases into our lives. When Abraham found birds swooping on his sacrifice attempting to steal it, he chased them away. Genesis 15:10–11: *"Then he brought all these to [God]....And when the vultures came down on the carcasses, Abram drove them away."*

Why Make Vows?

People often make vows, whether they are in the form of promises, signed contracts, or simple everyday financial decisions. There are good reasons why Christians should make vows:

1. **So that we will act**. Once we state our intention and determination to give to God, we become accountable to what we have said. This leads to disciplined living, the fear of God, and the assurance of receiving blessing through keeping the promises we make to God.

2. **Discipline**. Once we have made a promise to do something, we discipline ourselves in a way that we might not have without having made the promise.

3. **Public example**. A vow gives context to our Christianity. 1 Chronicles 29:5: *"Who then is willing to consecrate himself this day to the LORD?"*

4. **So God will act on our behalf**. Numbers 21:2–3: *"So Israel made a vow to the LORD, and said, 'If You will indeed deliver this people into my hand, then I*

will utterly destroy their cities.' And the LORD listened to the voice of Israel and delivered up the Canaanites, and they utterly destroyed them and their cities."

5. **The Bible encourages us to make vows to God**. Psalm 76:11: *"Make vows to the LORD your God, and pay them; Let all who are around Him bring presents to Him who ought to be feared."*

Let Your Yes Be Yes, and Your No, No

In Matthew 5:37, Jesus tells us that we are not to swear by God or any other thing, but to simply keep our word, without having to affirm our promises with an added oath—as if that will make us do what we say we'll do.

As disciples of Christ, we are people who make promises and *keep them*. In fact, in Psalm 15:4, the psalmist tells us that the person who walks with God *"swears to his own hurt."* This refers to making a promise only to realize later that it has become inconvenient to keep it, *and yet still keeping it.*

A minister once made an arrangement to come to our church. We prepared for his arrival and ministry in many different ways. I received a call the day he was meant to arrive, telling me, "The Lord has changed my plans, and I am unable to come." I refused to accept his backing out on his word as a man of God. I held him to his word and inferred that he had to come if he wanted to maintain a solid relationship with me and my church. They responded that they were surprised that I didn't seem to be very understanding of the reversal of their plans. The plain fact was, I wasn't very understanding at all, because it wasn't the "reversal of their plans," it was their canceling of a vow they had made to me.

The inability to adhere to one's word is nothing more than flaky Christianity. According to James 1:8, that type of person is double-minded and *"unstable in all his ways."*

———————

When we use subjective impressions, such as "God told me" or "I feel led" to break with the plainly understood, written Word of God, then we are opening ourselves to error. If it becomes difficult to continue with a commitment, whether it is inconvenient or painful to do so, the Word says we need to *stick with it anyway!* We are not to claim that God is telling us we are now released because we couldn't go through with it. That is why marriages in the ministry are falling apart. When we are married, we have made a vow to God that we will love our spouse for life. When the going gets rough—like all relationships do at times—we cannot claim that God is leading us now in another direction, and so break the marriage.

It is imperative that we always keep our word: God *always* keeps His!

Key #40

Reason Five: When We Give, All Grace Abounds

But this I say: He who sows sparingly will also reap sparingly, and he who sows bountifully will also reap bountifully. So let each one give as he purposes in his heart, not grudgingly or of necessity, for God loves a cheerful giver. And God is able to make all grace abound toward you, that you, always having all sufficiency in all things, may have an abundance for every good work. As it is written: "He has dispersed abroad, He has given to the poor; His righteousness endures forever."
—2 Corinthians 9:6–9

Paul appeals to the Corinthians to understand the laws of God. Abundant reaping comes from abundant sowing. Paul leads us into one of the most powerful Scriptures in the entire Bible. To the person who is an abundant, generous, cheerful, and purposeful giver, God will make *all* grace abound! Grace is favor with God. It is unlimited blessing. It is enabling power. It is all the gifts of God. It is the free, undeserved, unmerited, unearned blessing of God. Paul says that all there is of this grace is available to the cheerful, abundant giver. He then goes on to say that this grace will abound toward you. It will not just sneak up on you. It will not timidly come tapping on your door. It will not come in small measures, drips and drops, or tremulous occurrences. It will *abound* to you!

The purpose of this, Paul says, is so you will *"always* [have] *all sufficiency in all things."* That means it is the will of God for you and I to enjoy a complete sufficiency in every area of our lives at all times. Not just on payday. Not just when we get a bonus. Not just when our tax rebate comes in. Not just when we receive an inheritance. But *all the time!* Every Monday, Tuesday, Wednesday, Thursday, Friday, Saturday, and Sunday, in every month of the year,

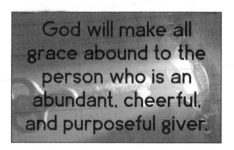

God will make all grace abound to the person who is an abundant, cheerful, and purposeful giver.

every year of our lives, for the rest of our lives—that is what *"always"* means! It also means that we will always have enough clothes, enough food, enough money, enough cars, enough houses, enough of everything that we need, all the time.

———◆———

Paul goes on to say that the purpose of always having this abundance is so that we can be engaged in *"every good work.*" When the offering for the new building comes by, we can get involved. Instead of thinking, "I've already given my tithes and an offering," we can rejoice because we have another opportunity for giving and sowing. This also means that when we meet someone in need, we have an abundance for her so we can meet her need. We can continuously involve ourselves in every good work as abundant sowers in the kingdom of God.

God Will Supply Seed to the Sower

Now may He who supplies seed to the sower, and bread for food, supply and multiply the seed you have sown and increase the fruits of your righteousness.
(2 Corinthians 9:10)

Paul appeals to the Corinthians to understand that God will supply. Once you've made the commitment to be a sower, God will supply the seed for sowing. If your need exceeds the money you have, then the money you do have is seed for sowing so that God is able to continuously supply your need.

Sowers are people who have lifestyles of sowing. They are not just one-time or once a week sowers, but at all times these people are looking for opportunities to give, to bless, and to sow seed into others.

Many people see the supply of God as a pie: There's is a slice for the tithe, then a slice for the rent, another slice for food, another for bills, one for other expenses—and that's it, the pie's all gone! But God is not a slice of pie! He's an inexhaustibly abundant river of never-ending supply that never runs dry. The supply of God is fluid: As His supply flows through us, it also flows to us, in a perpetual cycle of sowing, planting, harvesting, and reaping.

No Mere Paupers

The earth is not running dry. Globally, over the next few decades, the human race will extract from the earth tens of billions of dollars worth of copper, gold, silver, aluminum, iron, tin, zinc, and lead and trillions of dollars worth of coal. We will produce trillions worth of oil, barley, corn, rice, pork, wheat, and beef. These are just the current natural resources of the planet God made for us to reside upon. And that doesn't even begin to include the vast wealth coming from production, machinery, real estate, computers, transaction fees, banking, commerce, trading, and all the other means of wealth generation that God has placed on earth.

None of those reserves of wealth were made to go into the hands of the enemies of God to finance opposition to His work here on earth! This is God's earth, not the devil's! The wealth of the planet that He has created belongs in the hands of His children! All the great wedges of gold, all the diamonds, and all the oil has been placed in the earth for the children of God to inherit and utilize.

The Law of the Harvest

By this My Father is glorified, that you bear much fruit; so you will be My disciples.   (John 15:8)

There is no lack whatsoever to the abundance of riches God has in store for His children. The key to releasing this abundance into our lives is *giving*. Since the beginning of the world, God planned to supply abundance for His children by placing all kinds of incredible resources in the earth. Yet, because of the *poverty mind-set* that prevails, with which the devil has duped the church, many Christians actually feel that it is wrong to prosper! What a sad, unnecessary, and unbiblical way of thinking.

Poverty is more a *state of mind* than a state of life. People with a poverty mind-set walk around shops for half a day comparing prices only to save themselves a few dollars. If we think that saving five or ten dollars is worth half a day's effort, then we are living in a poverty mind-set.

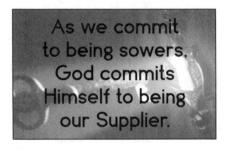

As we commit to being sowers, God commits Himself to being our Supplier.

Refusing to eat things out of the mini-bar in your hotel room and instead walking five blocks to get a Snickers bar for twenty cents less is a poverty mind-set. Eating everything on your plate even though you're stuffed full and feeling uncomfortable (and heck, you paid for it didn't you!) is a poverty mind-set. Buying cheap clothes that fall apart or wear out more quickly and aren't as nice to wear as more expensive garments that look and feel great and last twice as long is a poverty mind-set. Those types of choices reveal the operation of a mind-set of poverty.

Some people take that mind-set even further by doing such things as not making full customs declarations in order to avoid paying duty. It is amazing that people are willing to sacrifice their integrity just to save a few bucks. Money is nowhere near as important as honesty and integrity.

All we achieve when we do those things is to reinforce a poverty mind-set and a religious spirit (which always work together). People dominated by that kind of thinking imagine they are meant to live a life of scraping by. They think that this somehow pleases God. But *nothing* could be further from the truth!

As we make a commitment to be sowers in this world, God Himself makes a commitment to be our Supplier. That is a law of the harvest, a law of the kingdom—*sowers receive abundant supply!*

KEY #41

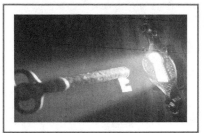

REASON SIX:
THAT GOD BE GLORIFIED

*For the administration of this service not only
supplies the needs of the saints, but also is
abounding through many thanksgivings to God,
while, through the proof of this ministry,
they glorify God for the obedience of
your confession to the gospel of Christ.*
—2 Corinthians 9:12–13

The ultimate result of sacrificial offerings is that God receives glory. When people step out in faith and give generously, God is glorified. People who give are worshippers—they glorify God with their generosity. The receivers of the gift glorify God for supplying their need so abundantly. Onlookers glorify God with wonder over the provision of God. Nonbelievers are compelled to at least ponder the workings of God and His people.

REASONS TO GIVE SACRIFICIAL OFFERINGS TO GOD

The book of Malachi is often quoted in relation to tithing and offering. However, the major theme of the prophet is *the glory of God*. Malachi tells the priests and the people that they must *"lay it to heart"* (Malachi 2:2 KJV) to give glory to God. It is our high-quality offerings that bring full glory to our awesome God.

> *This is what the LORD spoke, saying: "By those who come near Me I must be regarded as holy; and before all the people **I must be glorified**."*
> (Leviticus 10:3, emphasis added)

LIVING IN GOD'S ECONOMY

KEY #42

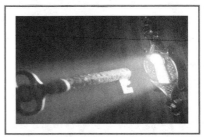

A STEP OF FAITH

The steps of a good man are ordered by the LORD,
and He delights in his way.
—Psalm 37:23

B ringing our pledge to the Lord is a *step of faith*. As we commit to give a certain sum of money, we may be left lacking in another area. Thus, it is a sacrifice and a step of faith whereby we believe that God will supply our need.

John Bunyan, author of the classic book *Pilgrim's Progress*, was regularly shut away in prison because he would not renounce his faith and cease his preaching. He lived in constant overwhelming grief because his family was bereft of their father. He had to make a sacrifice for his faith. Yet, it was in prison that he wrote his classic best-seller.

Our greatest achievements will come out of our greatest sacrifices. God sacrificed His Son for the sins of the world. The return from that one act is beyond description or comprehension.

Taking a step of faith releases the power of God. Many of us *say* we believe God but never *step out* beyond what we can see. It is only when we step out and put ourselves in a realm where we are standing on nothing but the promises of God (and not on our own assured finances) that we will see the miraculous supply of the Lord.

We are called to a "walk" in faith. A walk is a series of steps. A step is a decision. A walk, therefore, is a series of decisions we make. It is in the initial step of faith that the miracle happens. Time and again, God calls on people to take *a step of faith* so that miracles will take place in their lives.

In John 4, Jesus simply tells the nobleman with the dying child to, *"Go your way."* The man believed Him *and went*, and his son was healed:

> *The nobleman said to Him, "Sir, come down before my child dies!" Jesus said to him, "Go your way; your son lives." So the man believed the word that Jesus spoke to him, and he went his way. And as he was now going down, his servants met him and told him, saying, "Your son lives!"* (John 4:49–51)

In Luke 17, Jesus tells the ten lepers to go and show themselves to the priests, that they were healed. But it wasn't until they began walking to the temple that they were healed. It was when they *took the step of faith* that the miracle took place:

> *"Go, show yourselves to the priests." And so it was that as they went, they were cleansed.* (Luke 17:14)

Jesus tells the paralyzed man lying on his bed to *take the step of faith* and begin to walk:

"But that you may know that the Son of Man has power on earth to forgive sins"; then He said to the paralytic, "Arise, take up your bed, and go to your house."   (Matthew 9:6)

Jesus told the man with the withered hand in the synagogue to *step forward* and stretch it out:

"Stretch out your hand." And he stretched it out, and it was restored as whole as the other.   (Matthew 12:13)

Joshua was told to *step into* the river Jordan to make it stop flowing. As he took that step of faith, the water stopped flowing and the Israelites crossed the Jordan to take the city of Jericho, and ultimately the entire land of Canaan:

And the feet of the priests who bore the ark dipped in the edge of the water...that the waters which came down from upstream stood still, and rose in a heap very far away.   (Joshua 3:15–16)

At the gate Beautiful, Peter and John commanded a man who was lame to *stand up and walk*, to take the step of faith. As he does so, he is healed:

Then Peter said, "Silver and gold I do not have, but what I do have I give you: In the name of Jesus Christ of Nazareth, rise up and walk."   (Acts 3:6)

Jesus called on Peter to *step out* of the security of the boat and walk on the water:

And Peter answered Him and said, "Lord, if it is You, command me to come to You on the water." So He said, "Come." And when Peter had come down out of the boat, he walked on the water to go to Jesus.
(Matthew 14:28–29)

This occurred during the fourth watch of the night, which began at three in the morning. That means that it was near sunrise, so the disciples had been struggling with the storm for almost the entire night, and yet they were only halfway across the lake.

Peter sought the Word of the Lord, which is where faith comes from, where we sense the guiding hand of God. As Christ came close to them, they were afraid because He had never come to them that way before, walking on water.

———

All of those people were asked to *take a step* <u>before</u> the evidence of a miracle was revealed to them! That's why it is called *the step of faith.*

The step of faith can be also a step of sacrifice. Possibly the greatest step of faith recorded in Scripture is Abraham's readiness to give up his beloved son Isaac. The story in Genesis 22 tells us that God asked Abraham to slay his son Isaac as an offering to Jehovah. Abraham is prepared to carry out God's instructions. He had waited one hundred years for this son, but now God wanted to know that Abraham would hold nothing back from his God.

Abraham was faced with a supremely confusing situation: God had promised that Isaac was the one through whom the promised Messiah would eventually come. Yet, Abraham displayed his faith even *before* he took his step of faith: Abraham told his servants that he *and the boy* would return from sacrificing on the mountain:

> *Abraham said to his young men, "Stay here with the donkey; the lad and I will go yonder and worship, and **we** will come back to you."*
>
> (Genesis 22:5, emphasis added)

Abraham did not offer one of his servants' children, or even Ishmael, but the son through whom he knew God was going to fulfill all of His promises.

Chrysostom, the early Christian historian, said concerning this moment in Abraham's life, "The things of God seemed to fight against the things of God, and faith fought with faith, and the commandment fought with the promise."

Abraham did a lot of thinking as he trudged up that mountain, followed by his son and porters. God had told him that He would bless him through his only son Isaac. But now Jehovah was telling the patriarch to give his son to God—to *kill him*, as a sacrifice! Abraham chose to step out in faith in his sacrifice. He knew that the only way the promise and the requirement from God could be fulfilled was that God would either raise his boy from the dead or provide another sacrifice instead—that was the only way Abraham could discern that he could both carry out the commandment and still see God's word come to pass.

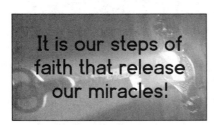

It is our steps of faith that release our miracles!

> *By faith Abraham, when he was tested, offered up Isaac, and he who had received the promises offered*

up his only begotten son, of whom it was said, "In Isaac your seed shall be called," concluding that God was able to raise him up, even from the dead.

(Hebrews 11:17–19)

What an exciting revelation that moment of clarity must have delivered to the aged prophet! *Yes, I will sacrifice the boy as God has instructed me...and I will watch as God raises the lad back to life.* This was a step of faith unprecedented in the history of the world.

Faith is that quality that enables us to give to God and know that we are not going to lose through the transaction—indeed, that we will greatly gain. It is our steps of faith that release our miracles!

KEY #43

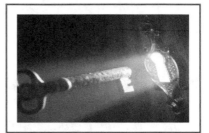

SACRIFICIAL GIVING PRODUCES ABUNDANCE

Bennett Cerf told a great story about a bus that was bumping along a country back road. In one of the seats sat a wispy old man, holding a bunch of fresh flowers. Across the aisle was a young girl whose eyes fell again and again to the flowers. The time eventually came when bus arrived at the old man's stop, and he prepared to exit the bus. Impulsively, he thrust the flowers into the girl's lap. "I can see you love the flowers," he explained, "and I think my wife would like for you to have them. I'll tell her I gave them to you." The girl accepted the flowers and watched as the old man got off the bus—and walked through the gate of a small cemetery.

A Widow's Sacrifice

And it happened after a while that the brook dried up, because there had been no rain in the land. Then the

*word of the LORD came to him, saying, "Arise, go to
Zarephath, which belongs to Sidon, and dwell there.
See, I have commanded a widow there to provide for
you." So he arose and went to Zarephath. And when
he came to the gate of the city, indeed a widow was
there gathering sticks. And he called to her and said,
"Please bring me a little water in a cup, that I may
drink." And as she was going to get it, he called to
her and said, "Please bring me a morsel of bread in
your hand." So she said, "As the LORD your God lives,
I do not have bread, only a handful of flour in a bin,
and a little oil in a jar; and see, I am gathering a couple of sticks that I may go in and prepare it for myself
and my son, that we may eat it, and die." And Elijah
said to her, "Do not fear; go and do as you have said,
but make me a small cake from it first, and bring
it to me; and afterward make some for yourself and
your son. For thus says the LORD God of Israel: "The
bin of flour shall not be used up, nor shall the jar of
oil run dry, until the day the LORD sends rain on the
earth." So she went away and did according to the
word of Elijah; and she and he and her household
ate for many days. The bin of flour was not used up,
nor did the jar of oil run dry, according to the word
of the LORD which He spoke by Elijah.*

(1 Kings 17:7–16)

In the passage above, Elijah is sent by God to the widow
of Zarephath. God had told the mighty prophet that He would
supply all of his food through this woman, even though the
land was going through a severe famine. In fact, judgment
had fallen on the kingdom of Ahab, and the famine had come

because of the praying and prophesying of Elijah. But Elijah wasn't living under that judgment. He was living right, and he was under the blessing of God.

When Elijah found the woman, she was ready to die. She had but one meager handful of flour left. Yet, the man of God instructed her to use a portion of it to bake some bread for him. That was an enormous request, because the woman had a hungry son. It is also enormous because the prophet was bold enough to ask a starving widow to give a piece of her only remaining food to him! Elijah was not starving. Ravens had previously miraculously fed him day and night by the brook Cherith. It would be easy to criticize the man of God for taking advantage of the woman's religious beliefs.

It was the type of story an investigative TV show would get a lot of mileage out of—a hot exposé on a supposedly greedy, self-absorbed preacher. Yet, the humble widow was ready to do whatever the mighty prophet of God asked. She baked a small cake and gave it to him. Immediately after he had eaten it, she went to the barrel of flour...and found it full to the top! From then on, no matter how much she took from it, it always refilled again.

This continuous miracle began with a widow's sacrifice. Most serious giving involves some form of sacrifice. There is always something else we can do with the money. Yet, when we give it to God, we trigger the beginning of miracles from heaven!

Isaac Sows in a Land of Famine

There was a famine in the land...and Isaac went to Abimelech king of the Philistines, in Gerar. Then the LORD appeared to him and said: "Do not go down to

Egypt: live in the land of which I shall tell you. Dwell in this land, and I will be with you and bless you." Then Isaac sowed in that land, and reaped in the same year a hundredfold; and the LORD blessed him. The man began to prosper, and continued prospering until he became very prosperous.

(Genesis 26:1–3; 12–13)

Isaac (whose name means "laughter") was the son of Abraham. He doesn't register in biblical history as a major figure. Possibly the most meaningful moment we can draw from his life is when he submits to his father on Mount Moriah, allowing himself to be bound and laid on the altar to be sacrificed. This prefigures exactly what Jesus did in laying down his life for the lost. Apart from this one mention, however, none  of his words or deeds are quoted by any minor or major prophets or New Testament writers. He is mentioned just once as placing a blessing on his children *"by faith"* (Hebrews 11:20). Yet, we read that he man became extraordinarily prosperous.

What caused this blessing of God to rest upon him was simply that he was the son of Abraham, with whom God had made a sweeping and magnificent covenant concerning the entire Hebrew nation. Part of that covenant was that God would bless the man so that he would prosper.

Abram was very rich in livestock, in silver, and in gold. (Genesis 13:2)

The promise God gave Abraham extended to his descendants, who would inherit the same blessing. In fact, it extended to the descendants of Abraham inheriting *the entire world!*

For the promise that he would be the heir of the world was not to Abraham or to his seed through the law, but through the righteousness of faith.   (Romans 4:13)

As long as Isaac stayed in the land of promise, he would receive the blessings of promise that had rested upon his father, for the blessing of God rested upon Abraham's son Isaac. The blessing rests on what we do—we are not blessed when we do nothing. If we fail to act, there is nothing for God to bless. Isaac still had to carry out the normal procedures of farming. He plowed his fields. He sowed the seed. He farmed his land.

Even though there was a famine in the land, it did not affect Isaac. Right up to his fence line the grass was green, the rain would fall, the crops were tall and healthy, and the sun would shine. Immediately over his fence line, the land of the Philistines was a drought-stricken dust bowl. Nothing was growing. There was no water, no sun, no crops, just dirt. The promise wasn't on the Philistines, it was on the offspring of Abraham.

The incredible news is that when we receive Jesus Christ, we not only become brothers of Jesus and children of God, but we also become inheritors of the awesome blessing of Abraham:

And if you are Christ's, then you are Abraham's seed, and heirs according to the promise....Now we, brethren, as Isaac was, are children of promise.
(Galatians 3:29; 4:28)

Nor are they all children because they are the seed of Abraham; but, "In Isaac your seed shall be called." That is, those who are the children of the flesh, these are not the children of God; but the children of the promise are counted as the seed. (Romans 9:7–8)

Giving Is Sowing

The New Testament contains at least two references to giving as being exactly the same as the sowing of seed (2 Corinthians 9:6, *"He who sows sparingly will also reap sparingly, and he who sows bountifully will also reap bountifully,"* and Galatians 6:7, *"Whatever a man sows, that he will also reap."*). The apostle Paul (who wrote both of these verses) is not attempting to give us an agricultural lesson. The context of both Scriptures concerns the giving of finances.

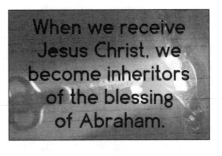

When we receive Jesus Christ, we become inheritors of the blessing of Abraham.

When we, like Isaac, sow into the kingdom through giving, we do it as inheritors of the blessing of Abraham. What God promised to Abraham also rests on us. So, just like Isaac, we are blessed in our efforts. Not because of anything special about ourselves, but because of the covenant that God made with Abraham and the promise that it would extend to his descendants.

What happened to Isaac will happen to us: He reaped a hundredfold in the same year!

KEY #44

GIVING THAT RELEASES MIRACLES

And my God shall supply all your need according to His riches in glory by Christ Jesus.
—Philippians 4:19

In the verse above, Paul tells the Philippians that his God is going to supply all of their needs according to His riches in glory by Christ Jesus. He is inspired by the Holy Spirit to speak this great promise to them because they have just sent Him an offering.

Jamieson, Fausset & Brown's Commentary makes a great note on this Bible verse:

> Paul says, "my God" to imply that God would reward their bounty to His servant, by "fully supplying"[*pleeroosei*, which means literally, to *fill to the full*] their every temporal and spiritual "need"

(2 Corinthians 9:8), even as they had "fully" supplied his "need" (Philippians 4:16, 18). My Master will fully repay you; I cannot. The Philippians invested their bounty well, since it got them such a return.[6]

In a phrase, they were going to reap what they had sown.

Recently in one of our Sunday night services, my assistant minister was giving the announcements and congratulated a young couple who had been married the day before. I was so surprised and impressed that they were in church when they would normally have been away on a honeymoon that I told them to come down to the front

Giving releases the miraculous!

and I'd give them a hundred dollars. They were embarrassed, but they came down anyway. Once they arrived, someone else ran out of the congregation and gave them some money. Then another person came and another and another. Pretty soon they had nearly $1,500 in their hands!

I thought that was all wonderful enough, but over the following week I heard all kinds of other details about the event. First, the reason they were not on a honeymoon was because they had no money for it. Second, just before they had been singled out in church, they had put their last $50 in the offering. The boy's mother, who had been cynical about our church, was at the back of the auditorium weeping as she witnessed the people of God blessing her son and

---

[6] http://www.site-berea.com/B/jfb/n11c4.html

new daughter-in-law. Others came to Christ that night as a result of seeing the love of God in action. God supplied this couple's need by acting in response to their giving to Him.

Henry Wadsworth Longfellow once said, "Give what you have. To someone, it may be better than you dare to think."

One of the most famous miracles in history began with a small boy's gift. In John 6:9, Andrew asks Jesus how they would be able to feed the multitudes in front of them. The answer came in a young man offering his lunch. Jesus blessed and broke the small amount of food. He then gave it to the disciples. As they gave what they had been given, the food multiplied so much that every person was fed to satisfaction.

Giving releases the miraculous!

KEY #45

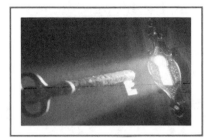

OFFERINGS ARE WARFARE

And I will rebuke the devourer for your sakes, so that he will not destroy the fruit of your ground.
—Malachi 3:11

T he devil hates offerings—not just because they will ultimately cause the people of God to prosper, but also because they contain spiritual power. In the New Testament, one of the most tangible things we can offer to God is our finances. Today, when we give with cash, check, credit or debit card, or electronic transfer, we are offering a material piece of our lives. In the Old Testament, the Israelites were required to offer physical sacrifices to God—whether it was grain offerings or animals.

───◆───

Throughout biblical history, when offerings were made correctly to God, the power of Satan was bound and the power of the Holy Spirit was released. When Elijah made his offering to God at the summit of Mount Carmel, the power of the devil over the people's lives was broken and they turned from devotion of the false god Baal to worshipping the living God, Jehovah. Immediately following this, Elijah prayed and there was a deluge of rain that broke a drought that had previously devastated the nation of Israel.

Protect Your Offerings

When Abraham made his offering to the Lord, he had to drive away the birds of the air because they were trying to steal the offering he was making:

> *And when the vultures came down on the carcasses, Abram drove them away.* (Genesis 15:11)

We must take aggressive action against anything that attempts to steal our offering to the Lord. Vultures of all kinds will swoop to take away what we have prepared for God. Abraham protected his offering from being consumed by other things. So must we. All too often, an urgent need, an unexpected invoice, a strong desire, or a friend's request threatens to take our tithe or our offering. As we remain committed to bringing the offering we have set apart for God, He will supply whatever we need for our own lives—including whatever threatened to steal our tithe.

Malachi says the very act of giving an offering causes God to rebuke the devourer:

> *And I will rebuke the devourer for your sakes, so that he will not destroy the fruit of your ground.*
> (Malachi 3:11)

The devourer here is not "it," but *"he,"* indicating a personality. In John 10:10, Jesus said the devil comes to kill, steal, and destroy. One of his intentions is to destroy the offerings that belong to the Lord. This is because they release a spiritual power, which, in effect, binds the works of the devil.

Malachi talks about the devil destroying *"the fruit of your ground."* Offerings to God have a direct influence on the levels of fruitfulness we will experience in our service to God. Fruitfulness is what the devil is most concerned about.

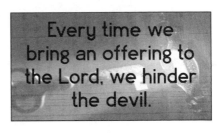

Every time we bring an offering to the Lord, we hinder the devil.

Our money can easily be seen as representing life. As we sacrificially give our lives to the Lord, we release a godly spiritual power that invokes blessing over our lives. Every time we bring an offering to the Lord, instead of the devil hindering us, we hinder the devil and block his workings in our lives.

RELEASING
BLESSINGS
TO OTHERS

KEY #46

WITHHOLDING

Do not withhold good from those who deserve it when it's in your power to help them.
—Proverbs 3:27 NLT

G od places abundance in our hands so we are able to bless others. If, however, we withhold that blessing, our possessions will be cursed.

There is one who scatters, yet increases more; and there is one who withholds more than is right, but it leads to poverty. (Proverbs 11:24)

Visible blessing is no accident. It comes because of private generosity. It comes because of diligence, integrity, and good stewardship of what we have been entrusted with.

When we employ the services of another, we are to pay them promptly. James warned that withholding people's due wages only invites catastrophe.

Indeed the wages of the laborers who mowed your fields, which you kept back by fraud, cry out; and the cries of the reapers have reached the ears of the Lord of Sabaoth. (James 5:4)

Do not say to your neighbor, "Go, and come back, and tomorrow I will give it," when you have it with you.
(Proverbs 3:28)

Withholding things from those to whom they are due is the best way to cause God to withhold from you!

KEY #47

HONOR GOD'S SERVANTS WITH GENEROUS GIVING

T he Bible tells us that we must give to those who teach us the Word of God:

Let him who is taught the word share in all good things with him who teaches. Do not be deceived, God is not mocked; for whatever a man sows, that he will also reap. For he who sows to his flesh will of the flesh reap corruption, but he who sows to the Spirit will of the Spirit reap everlasting life.

(Galatians 6:6–8)

When we are fed the Word of God, we are to bless those who minister the Word to us. When we eat at a restaurant, we don't eat and then leave without paying. We wouldn't even get out the door! If we ask for some bread at the local bakery and take it without paying, the owner will chase us down. No matter how sincere our protest may be, we have to pay.

We could tell the baker we want to support the small bread shop down the road or the new bakery that is just starting, but none of these reasons will be acceptable.

Where we are fed is where we should give. From whom we receive is to whom we should give. This is not just a New Testament or Old Testament concept; it is found in both testaments. Those who are called to minister spiritual things are to be supported by those they minister to.

> *If we have sown spiritual things for you, is it a great thing if we reap your material things? If others are partakers of this right over you, are we not even more? Nevertheless we have not used this right, but endure all things lest we hinder the gospel of Christ. Do you not know that those who minister the holy things eat of the things of the temple, and those who serve at the altar partake of the offerings of the altar? Even so the Lord has commanded that those who preach the gospel should live from the gospel.*
>
> (1 Corinthians 9:11–14)

Adam Clarke, in his commentary,[7] declares it "unjust" to expect that a person should give up his life and his time to teach us the Word of God and then not think that we should contribute to his support.

Ministers are to give themselves to the teaching, reading and study of the Scriptures and not to become entangled in the affairs of this life (2 Timothy 2:4). These ministers of the Word of God are not to be engaged in business affairs as a way of life, struggling daily to generate income. They are

---

[7] *Adam Clarke's Bible Commentary,* http://www.godrules.net/library/clark/clarke3joh1.htm

to be bringing God to the people He has called them to minister to. This is the call God has placed on their lives. If they become distracted with tasks not related to their calling, then they will compromise the call upon their lives. That is why those who are not called to a ministerial lifestyle are to support those who are.

> *If you send them forward on their journey in a manner worthy of God, you will do well, because they went forth for His name's sake, taking nothing from the Gentiles. We therefore ought to receive such, that we may become fellow workers for the truth.*
>
> (3 John 1:6–8)

Adam Clarke says of the verse above: "Those congregations of Christians are ever found to prize the gospel most, and profit most by it, who bear all expenses incident to it, and vice versa."

The Living Bible translates 3 John 1:6–8 as follows:

> *They have told the church here of your friendship and your loving deeds. I am glad when you send them on their way with a generous gift. For they are traveling for the Lord and take neither food, clothing, shelter, nor money from those who are not Christians, even though they have preached to them. So we ourselves should take care of them in order that we may become partners with them in the Lord's work.*

The generosity of a gift is measured against the culture we live in. A generous gift is a *"manner worthy of God"* gift.

Those who are not called to preach and teach the Word can partner with those who are by blessing them generously.

That is how God looks after these men and women. They receive no help from the world, so we in the church must be their source of supply. When we *"receive"* these ministers (literally, "support," "under- write," "undertake to care for"), we become partners with them in what they are accomplish- ing in God's kingdom. When we support ministries, we are con- sidered by God to be fulfilling the same ministry as those who

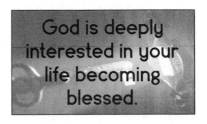

God is deeply interested in your life becoming blessed.

are reaching the lost for Christ and building up the church. Thus, we should bless those who minister the Word and Spir- it with a generosity that reflects the attitude of God Himself toward His faithful servants.

The Prophet's Reward

> *He who receives a prophet in the name of a prophet*
> *shall receive a prophet's reward. And he who receives*
> *a righteous man in the name of a righteous man shall*
> *receive a righteous man's reward.*   (Matthew 10:41)

Helping a ministry to achieve its God-given purpose causes us to be included in the rewards that ministry re- ceives. We can expect to receive the same rewards God has planned for it. In fact, in the third letter of John (which is addressed to Gaius), John pronounced health and prosperity over Gaius because of the prosperity of his soul. The abun- dance of his soul was manifested in the way he looked after the itinerant ministers. The generosity and abundant hospi- tality of Gaius were legendary. Traveling ministers brought reports back to the church at Ephesus of how well they had been looked after by Gaius. They testified that it felt like they had been looked after in a manner worthy of God.

———◆———

It is hard to find Jesus condemning the idea of giving in order to receive something back. Well-meaning Christians often argue that we should give, expecting nothing in return. This sounds like a far more sincere and pious attitude toward giving than one where we give expecting God to reward us. But the general tone of Scripture *encourages* us to give in such a way that our reward will be greater! Jesus is saying that if you look after a prophet—not just as an ordinary person but also as an anointed person of God—then you will receive the same kind of reward that the prophet receives.

———◆———

God is deeply interested in your life becoming blessed, and so He reveals the pathways to that blessing. A major stepping-stone in the pathway to the blessing of God is to honor His servants with generous giving!

KEY #48

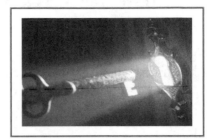

A LIFE OF GIVING

Do not be deceived, God is not mocked; for whatever a man sows, that he will also reap. For he who sows to his flesh will of the flesh reap corruption, but he who sows to the Spirit will of the Spirit reap everlasting life. And let us not grow weary while doing good, for in due season we shall reap if we do not lose heart. Therefore, as we have opportunity, let us do good to all, especially to those who are of the household of faith.
—Galatians 6:7–10

When we give to ministers, it is the same as sowing seed. In this light, God will not be mocked, which means He will not disappoint. People will not be able to mock God and say they gave to support His ministers or to His work and were left penniless because of it.

Every action causes a response. In the realm of sowing and reaping, Scripture assures us that whatever we sow is what we will reap. The great scientist Isaac Newton expressed this principle in his famous third law, "For every action there is an equal and opposite reaction."

Paul says that when we sow to the flesh we will reap corruption. Since this is said in the context of teaching on the giving of money, it is reasonable to assume that Paul is implying that if we fail to give, then we are sowing to the flesh; but if we are faithful to give, then we are sowing to the Spirit.

This is obvious if we stop to consider that when we support a preacher of the Word of God, we are supporting the work of the Holy Spirit because the preacher is engaged in building the church, in preaching the Word of God, and in training men and women for ministry. When we give to a minister who is doing these things, we are sowing to the work of the Spirit.

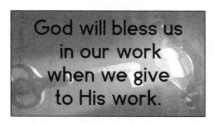

God will bless us in our work when we give to His work.

It is inevitable that God will bless us in our work when we give to His work. He will ensure that we reap as we have sown. However, this reaping is far broader than we imagine: It is not confined to our finances. Paul says that we will reap *"everlasting life"*—a life that is *inextinguishable!* People who give and support the life of the Spirit in the earth will reap that same life into their own. Generous people tend to be energetic. They are fired up and enthusiastic about life. They don't give up easily. They are inspired, thinking of new ways to bless and to create opportunities for themselves and for others.

The practice of giving to ministers is described by Paul as *"doing good."* He tells us to *"not grow weary"* in doing this. There are times when it is easy to become discouraged because we cannot see the harvest. Like any sowing process, there is always a period of time between the sowing and the reaping. This can seem a lot longer than we might want it to be.

When it comes to spiritual matters, the harvest can be very different in its timings than the natural world. Sometimes we can reap quickly; at other times the harvest seems to take far longer than anticipated. But it will come; the Word of God assures us of this. The only condition (other than giving in the first place) is that we *do not grow weary.* In other words, never lose heart and give up on giving. There will usually be a point of time when we feel like giving up on what we are doing. It may seem as though the results have not come through as we had expected. But they will come! We have God's word on it.

Continuing generosity will always increase your sowing and will provide a perfect spiritual climate for your harvest!

A Kingdom Mentality

Paul tells us that when we are given the opportunity to do good (which, in this context, means *giving*), we must apply this to all people. We may have special people whom we feel we want to single out to give to, but God does not want us to display partiality. Rather, we should take advantage of every opportunity to give whenever one presents itself. By the very fact that Paul says, *"especially those who are of the household of faith,"* he implies that we should also be engaged in giving to those who are not in the kingdom.

＊＊＊

When we get saved, our motivation in life must change from getting to giving. We live to give, not to get. When the word *opportunity* is mentioned, most of us focus on the benefits that could come to us. However, Paul uses the word *opportunity* in the context of an opportunity to *give*. He sees our lives as being conducted so that we are people who are constantly seeking to give to others, not to receive from them. This is a *kingdom mentality.* It is revolutionary. It is entirely different from the world. Yet it is also the key to your reaping a mighty harvest.

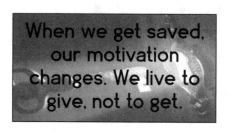

When we get saved, our motivation changes. We live to give, not to get.

The proper behavior for the believer is to bless with *"all good things"* (Galatians 6:6) those who teach them the Word. This includes finances, accommodations, food, clothing, and recreations—anything that is good for the minister of the Word.

Paul makes a statement that includes both a warning and a promise. Whichever way we respond to being taught the Word, we will be affected. If we fail to give to teachers of the Word of God after they have taught us, then we are considered to be sowing to the flesh. This is because we have yielded to the selfishness of our flesh and have justified to ourselves why we are not contributing to the ministry from which we have been receiving. Paul warns that this will cause corruption in our lives. When we strengthen our flesh, we only strengthen its negative consequences in our lives.

When we contribute to teachers of the Word of God, we are sowing to the Spirit. The work of the Holy Spirit is to spread the Word of God. He works through ministers to accomplish this. When we support those ministers He has chosen, we are giving to the Holy Spirit. He therefore gives back to us *"everlasting life"*; in other words, energy, motivation, health, and life that are unquenchable. The miser has no such promise. He can expect only corruption, decay, and lifeless days void of true peace and blessings.

KEY #49

LENDING

The LORD your God will bless you as he has promised. You will lend money to many nations but will never need to borrow!
—Deuteronomy 15:6 NLT

God has always intended that His people prosper so much that they will not need to borrow money. In fact, His purpose is that His people would have so much that they would be able to loan to others and thus *prosper.*

The Scripture regards those who need to borrow money as poor. Our modern world has so normalized debt that we find it virtually impossible to imagine life without it. If we are ever to be released from our deepening mind-set of indebtedness, then we desperately need to renew our minds in this area. In fact, one of the curses God proclaimed on Israel if they failed to remain true to Him is that they would have to borrow money from other nations. His blessing was that they would have such abundance they would be able to loan to others, while the curse was exactly the opposite: Israel would be the borrowers.

> *They shall lend to you, not you to them! They shall be the head and you shall be the tail!*
> (Deuteronomy 28:44 TLB)

Blessing comes with responsibilities. We are not blessed simply for personal benefit. We are blessed in order to *become a blessing*. One of the ways we can be a blessing is by loaning to others. God's intention is that we have enough to loan others in a fair and helpful way so they are blessed and can accomplish their dreams.

> *All goes well for the generous man who conducts his business fairly.*
> (Psalm 112:5 TLB)

The promise to those who do this is that the lender will enjoy a life that goes well. The assumption here is that we have enough to loan out to others.

———

Some people in our church are involved in arranging micro loans to people in developing nations. At present, they have seven hundred and fifty thousand loans out. All the loans are small in size, but in the recipients' world, the amounts are enough to be able to get them set up in a viable business. Their dignity remains intact as they receive not just charity, but a responsible business proposition, the ability to earn an income, and the opportunity to repay the money. Through the disciplines they learn, they are able to maintain a healthy, thriving business. This is generosity manifested in loaning, not just in giving.

KEY #50

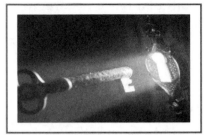

BUILDING GOD'S HOUSE

Thus speaks the LORD of hosts, saying: "This people says, 'The time has not come, the time that the Lord's house should be built.'"
—Haggai 1:2

aggai the prophet, born in captivity in Babylon, proph-esied to those returning to Israel in the year 520 BC that they were meant to be building the house of God. But they required encouragement in order to fulfill the call of God. Both Haggai and Zechariah revived the people to the work of building the house of God.

Fourteen years had lapsed since they had begun re-building, but all they had accomplished was to remove the rubble of the previously destroyed temple and to lay the first foundation of the new one. They had encountered op-position from the moment they began building. Eventually, even the king himself opposed their efforts, and the work was stopped.

However, the new king, Darius, endorsed the building program, so all that remained was for the people to revive their efforts in the building of the temple. But the Israelites had grown lax and were preoccupied with building their own homes, businesses, and families. They had been easily turned aside from the work of God. They were justifying their position from a religious perspective, arguing that the seventy years of captivity in Babylon also applied to the timing of building the temple. According to them, there were still two years of the prophecy to go. Their interpretation of prophecy was incorrect. The presence of the new king had removed all previous obstacles, and God wanted them to build.

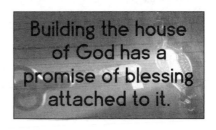

Building the house of God has a promise of blessing attached to it.

When people do not want to deny truth and yet do not want to respond to God, timing is the most commonly used excuse—"it is not yet God's timing," they claim. Even today, too many people use this excuse to avoid obedience to God.

Scottish theologian William Scroggie, in his book, *The Unfolding Drama of Redemption*, says concerning Haggai 1:2: "If we wait until the devil is agreeable to spiritual progress, we shall make none at all."

Jamieson, Fausset & Brown's Commentary says:

Ingenious in their excuses, they pretended that the interruption in their work caused by their enemies was proof that it was not yet the proper time; whereas their real motive was selfish dislike of the trouble, expense, and danger from enemies.[8]

---

[8] http://www.studylight.org/com/jfb/view.cgi?book=hag&chapter=001

The prophets Haggai and Zechariah dismantled this false, convenient refuge of delay and admonished the people to recommence work on the temple immediately.

Is it time for you yourselves to dwell in your paneled houses, and this temple to lie in ruins? Now therefore, thus says the LORD of hosts: "Consider your ways!"
(Haggai 1:4–5)

The prophet challenged the people to ponder whether they had prospered through focusing on the building of their own houses at the sacrifice of building God's house. Had they escaped poverty by not building the house of God and keeping their money to themselves? The question the prophet put to them is, *have they cheated God, or themselves?*

You have sown much, and bring in little; you eat, but do not have enough; you drink, but you are not filled with drink; you clothe yourselves, but no one is warm; and he who earns wages, earns wages to put into a bag with holes. Thus says the LORD of hosts: "Consider your ways! Go up to the mountains and bring wood and build the temple, that I may take pleasure in it and be glorified," says the LORD.   (Haggai 1:6–8)

The plain fact was that the temple was to be built to bring pleasure to God. It was to be built as a place where people could bring their worship, prayers, and sacrifices to God and find peace with Him. It was to be an altar of sacrifice and worship. It was to be a place for ministers to be chosen and made useful to God.

The people had hoped to become wealthy. Their vision was for much, but they received only little because their primary vision was for themselves and not for God.

The prophet continued:

"...and when you brought it home, I blew it away. Why?" says the LORD of hosts. "Because of My house that is in ruins, while every one of you runs to his own house." (Haggai 1:9)

The pursuit of our lives should not be to look after our own interests at the expense of God's house. The Bible assures us that such an attitude will cause what we bring home to be blown away—and worse:

Therefore the heavens above you withhold the dew, and the earth withholds its fruit. For I called for a drought on the land and the mountains, on the grain and the new wine and the oil, on whatever the ground brings forth, on men and livestock, and on all the labor of your hands. Then Zerubbabel the son of Shealtiel, and Joshua the son of Jehozadak, the high priest, with all the remnant of the people, obeyed the voice of the LORD their God, and the words of Haggai the prophet, as the LORD their God had sent him; and the people feared the presence of the LORD. (Haggai 1:10–12)

However, when the people finally determined to get their priorities right and to revive their hearts for the house of the Lord, God immediately spoke to them and encouraged them with the fact that He was with them:

Then Haggai, the Lord's messenger, spoke the Lord's message to the people, saying, "I am with you, says the lord." So the Lord stirred up the spirit of Zerubbabel the son of Shealtiel, governor of Judah, and

*the spirit of Joshua the son of Jehozadak, the high
priest, and the spirit of all the remnant of the people;
and they came and worked on the house of the Lord
of hosts, their God.* (Haggai 1:13–14)

The leaders prepared the way, and the people were stirred
to get the work done and to see victory at all costs. Once they
put God first, success came to their work for God—and their
personal circumstances enjoyed success, as well.

———◆———

The most incredible aspect of these passages in Haggai
is the twofold promise of blessing: First, it is clear from the
Scripture that when we give to God, we begin a process of
blessing into our lives; and second, it is clear that building
the house of God has a promise of blessing attached to it.
When we become engaged in giving, and that giving is for
the building of the house of God, then we are doubly guaran-
teed by the Lord Himself of bountiful blessings!

KEY #51

MISSION GIVING

How then shall they call on Him in whom they have not believed? And how shall they believe in Him of whom they have not heard? And how shall they hear without a preacher? And how shall they preach unless they are sent?
—Romans 10:14–15

Jesus, the greatest evangelist this world has ever seen, commissioned the church with the incredible task of preaching the gospel to the ends of the earth. That is no small task. There are six billion people in the world today—twice the number there was just thirty years ago. The earth's population is multiplying at a staggering rate, and the church is called on by God to bring these teeming billions to Christ. God has also determined that this should happen through the preaching of the gospel.

We need thousands and thousands of preachers to be released into the world to bring the gospel to the millions of people who are yet to be reached for Christ.

Charles Spurgeon said, in *Lectures to My Students on the Art of Preaching*, "Not only must something be done to evangelize the millions, but everything must be done."

When we arrive at church next Sunday, there will be one million more lost people in the world than there were when we arrived last Sunday. Some 155,000 people will die around the world in the next 24 hours. Most of them will not know Christ as their Savior. Roughly 108 people per minute (approximately two every second) are going to hell! A line made up of all the lost people in the world would circle the earth *thirty times*. This line grows at the rate of *twenty miles per day!* Every year, the world population increases by over 74 million—that's more than twice as fast as the death rate.

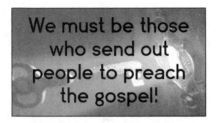

We must be those who send out people to preach the gospel!

Two out of every three Christians accept Christ before the age of eighteen. We must support every effort we can to reach youth around the world. The world is reverting to heathenism thirty times faster than it is being evangelized— even though approximately one hundred and fifty thousand people find Christ as their Savior every day. Countless millions are still lost and without Jesus. We are not sending out enough people to reap. But the devil is!

A Sinking World

A ship's officer who survived the sinking of the Titanic in 1912, died a year after the catastrophe. His last words were, "We must get them all into the lifeboats." The sense of duty that burned in that man's soul from that tragedy stayed with him until his death. The saving of some did not make him indifferent to the loss of others. His only thought was to get all men, women, and children on board into the lifeboats. There were approximately 2,200 people aboard the Titanic on her maiden voyage. The ship carried only twenty lifeboats, with a total capacity of 1,100 people. There were 1,517 lives lost and only 705 saved...because there were not enough lifeboats.

Are we Christians sending out enough lifeboats to a sinking world—a world sinking into hell? It is imperative that we support those going out to start new churches and evangelize the masses. That is the highest purpose of God on the entire planet! When we put our resources behind evangelizing, we will find ourselves so blessed from heaven that we are able to sow more into the harvest.

Any church not obeying or supporting the Great Commission is failing in its purpose, no matter what else it does. We must be those who send out people to preach the gospel!

KEY #52

BLESSING THE POOR

He who gives to the poor will not lack, but he who hides his eyes will have many curses.
—Proverbs 28:27

There are numerous Scriptures telling us to give to those who suffer from poverty in this life. This represents God's people bringing relief at a grassroots level, rather than waiting for government institutions to carry out such work. We are to be mindful of the poor in such a way that we give them practical help, not just some religious words of comfort. The Word is clear: We are to feed the hungry, clothe the naked, and provide shelter for the needy. And the reason is not purely to evangelize people: We are called to provide whether the people we help come to the Lord or not. It is mercy, compassion, and help *with no strings attached*.

Those who bless the poor will never lack in their own lives; they will enjoy the abundance of God.

One of the great reasons God blesses us is so we can be an expression of His heart to the suffering.

One who increases his possessions by usury and extortion gathers it for him who will pity the poor.
(Proverbs 28:8)

Those who increase their wealth by wicked means will lose it to those who are giving money to the poor. This is a principle of God in the earth, an unavoidable law. When we bless the poor, wealth from those who have practiced extortion will begin flowing into our world like a river.

He who has pity on the poor lends to the Lord, and He will pay back what he has given. (Proverbs 19:17)

When we bless the poor, we are blessing the Lord. Jesus told us that whatever we do to others who are suffering, we do to Him. We never lose by giving to the poor. God will ensure that whatever we give to those who are poor will return to us. The return of money is a small thing compared to the enlarging of the soul through having compassion for those who are struggling in life.

He who has a generous eye will be blessed, for he gives of his bread to the poor. (Proverbs 22:9)

We are not considered generous by heaven unless we have shared the resources of our lives with the poor. God pours out great blessings on the heads of those who remember the disadvantaged, the vulnerable, the marginalized, and the forgotten. We are to be the expression of the Father in the earth. When we bless these people, we are showing them the love of God.

If you help the poor, you are lending to the LORD—and he will repay you! (Proverbs 19:17 NLT)

Whoever gives to the poor will lack nothing. But a curse will come upon those who close their eyes to poverty. (Proverbs 28:27 NLT)

Oh, the joys of those who are kind to the poor. The LORD rescues them in times of trouble. The LORD protects them and keeps them alive. He gives them prosperity and rescues them from their enemies. The LORD nurses them when they are sick and eases their pain and discomfort. (Psalm 41:1–3 NLT)

God calls on us to bless those outside our lives. We are not called to be poor. We are called to work hard and prosper so we will have an abundance, in order to be a blessing to those who have nothing. This is one of the highest purposes of God that we can fulfill.

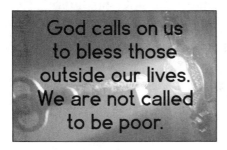

God calls on us to bless those outside our lives. We are not called to be poor.

In Ephesians 4:28, Paul tells the Ephesians that those who used to steal are to steal no more but rather to work hard so they have something to give.

The story of the good Samaritan, in Luke 10:30–35, continues to teach us today about caring for people. However, this story could never have happened if the Samaritan was not wealthy. Not only did the Samaritan put the half-dead man on his mount, he also took him to the local inn and told the proprietor to provide care for the man until he became well, and that when he returned, he would pay the entire bill. How many of us can take a half-dead person to a hospital, tell the doctors to do whatever it takes to make the person healthy again, and be able to pay the entire bill? Not without substantial finances!

The apostle Paul made the same inference in writing to his friend Philemon about his runaway slave Onesimus. The legal penalty a slave had to pay for running away was death. This slave had probably also stolen from his master when he ran. He had ended up in Rome, where Paul met him and led him to Christ. Paul sent Onesimus back home to Philemon, with a letter and an offer: *"But if he has wronged you or owes anything, put that on my account"* (Philemon 1:18). Paul had to have plenty of money to cover that very large bill.

IN CONCLUSION

REVIVAL AND GENEROSITY

C harles Finney, the American lawyer-turned-preacher who was known for his strong preaching on holiness, also discovered that revival followed generous congregations. He wrote:

> As I have gone from place to place working for revival, I have always found that churches are blessed in proportion to their liberality. Where they support the gospel and give generously to God's treasury, they have been blessed both spiritually and materially. But where they are stingy and allow the pastor to preach for little or nothing, the church is cursed instead of blessed. I have also found it generally true that young converts are most inclined to join churches making liberal efforts to support the gospel.[9]

Throughout Bible history, a revival of joy comes when great offerings are given.

> *The people rejoiced over the offerings, for they had given freely and wholeheartedly to the LORD, and King David was filled with joy.* (1 Chronicles 29:9 NLT)

Joy and generosity always go together. In fact, the word *miser* is at the root of the word *miserable*. People clutching on to their possessions will never discover the joy of a free, giving spirit.

The most important key to gaining and maintaining financial success in your life is that you *give generously!*

---

[9] Charles G. Finney, *Lectures on Revival* (Minneapolis, Minn.: Bethany House Publishers, 1988), 159.

ABOUT THE AUTHOR

Phil Pringle is the senior minister of Christian City Church Oxford Falls, in Sydney, Australia, and the founder and president of Christian City Church International (C3i). Originally from New Zealand, Phil and his wife, Christine, started Christian City Church (CCC) in 1980.

From small beginnings, CCC has grown to become one of the largest, most influential churches in Australia. The CCC movement consists of well over one hundred and seventy churches spread throughout the world. The entire movement of vibrant churches was birthed as a result of Phil Pringle's leadership and vision.

Phil's dynamic and relevant preaching has made him a much sought after speaker in both Christian and secular contexts. He is particularly noted for his insights on topics such as faith, leadership, the ministry of the Holy Spirit, church building, and kingdom principles of finance and giving.

Phil and his wife live in Sydney, Australia.

Faith:
Moving the Heart and the Hand of God
Phil Pringle

You are invited on a journey *into* faith so that you can live a life *of* faith. Author Phil Pringle reminds us of the vital principle that faith is what God responds to. Throughout the Scriptures, faith is highlighted as the necessary ingredient for a close relationship with God, meaningful service for Him, and a fulfilling life. If we are on the path of faith, then our destination is sure—a life saved by the work of Christ, the fulfillment of our God-given dreams on earth, and a joyful eternity with our heavenly Father. Let's get started on the journey!

ISBN: 0-88368-174-9 • Hardcover • 192 pages

You the Leader
Phil Pringle

Drawing from Scripture, personal experience, and the writings of both contemporary and historical leaders, pastor Phil Pringle offers practical insights into effective leadership that can be applied in every arena of life, not just inside church walls. As you examine the attributes of dynamic leaders and the kingdom principles that govern their lives, you will discover how to realize your personal leadership potential. Explore how to implement the vision God has instilled in you—and enjoy the process of becoming the leader He has called you to be!

ISBN: 0-88368-814-X • Hardcover • 320 pages

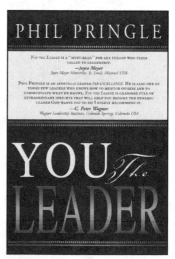

WHITAKER HOUSE
proclaiming the power of the Gospel through the written word
visit our website at www.whitakerhouse.com